For every kind of comput there is a SYBEX boc

All computer users learn in their own way. Some need straightforward and methodical explanations. Others are just too busy for this approach. But no matter what camp you fall into, SYBEX has a book that can help you get the most out of your computer and computer software while learning at your own pace.

Beginners generally want to start at the beginning. The **ABC's** series, with its step-by-step lessons in plain language, helps you build basic skills quickly. Or you might try our **Quick & Easy** series, the friendly, full-color guide.

The **Mastering** and **Understanding** series will tell you everything you need to know about a subject. They're perfect for intermediate and advanced computer users, yet they don't make the mistake of leaving beginners behind.

If you're a busy person and are already comfortable with computers, you can choose from two SYBEX series—**Up & Running** and **Running Start**. The **Up & Running** series gets you started in just 20 lessons. Or you can get two books in one, a step-by-step tutorial and an alphabetical reference, with our **Running Start** series.

Everyone who uses computer software can also use a computer software reference. SYBEX offers the gamut—from portable **Instant References** to comprehensive **Encyclopedias, Desktop References**, and **Bibles**.

SYBEX even offers special titles on subjects that don't neatly fit a category—like **Tips & Tricks**, the **Shareware Treasure Chests**, and a wide range of books for Macintosh computers and software.

SYBEX books are written by authors who are expert in their subjects. In fact, many make their living as professionals, consultants or teachers in the field of computer software. And their manuscripts are thoroughly reviewed by our technical and editorial staff for accuracy and ease-of-use.

So when you want answers about computers or any popular software package, just help yourself to SYBEX.

For a complete catalog of our publications, please write:

SYBEX Inc.
2021 Challenger Drive
Alameda, CA 94501
Tel: (510) 523-8233/(800) 227-2346 Telex: 336311
Fax: (510) 523-2373

SYBEX is committed to using natural resources wisely to preserve and improve our environment. As a leader in the computer book publishing industry, we are aware that over 40% of America's solid waste is paper. This is why we have been printing the text of books like this one on recycled paper since 1982.

This year our use of recycled paper will result in the saving of more than 15,300 trees. We will lower air pollution effluents by 54,000 pounds, save 6,300,000 gallons of water, and reduce landfill by 2,700 cubic yards.

SECRETS

OF

EFFECTIVE

GUI

DESIGN

SECRETS
OF
EFFECTIVE
GUI
DESIGN

Mark Minasi

San Francisco
Paris
Düsseldorf
Soest

 SYBEX®

DEVELOPMENTAL EDITOR: *Gary Masters*

EDITOR: *Guy Hart-Davis*

TECHNICAL EDITOR: *Michael J. Young*

BOOK DESIGNER: *Helen Bruno*

TECHNICAL ART: *Cuong Le*

SCREEN GRAPHICS: *John Corrigan*

PAGE LAYOUT AND TYPESETTING: *Len Gilbert*

PRODUCTION ASSISTANT/PROOFREADER: *Kristin Amlie*

INDEXER: *Nancy Guenther*

COVER DESIGNER: *Ingalls + Associates*

COVER PHOTOGRAPHER: *Mark Johann*

Screen reproductions produced with Collage Plus.

Collage Plus is a trademark of Inner Media Inc.

SYBEX is a registered trademark of SYBEX Inc.

TRADEMARKS: SYBEX has attempted throughout this book to distinguish proprietary trademarks from descriptive terms by following the capitalization style used by the manufacturer.

SYBEX is not affiliated with any manufacturer.

Every effort has been made to supply complete and accurate information. However, SYBEX assumes no responsibility for its use, nor for any infringement of the intellectual property rights of third parties which would result from such use.

Library of Congress Card Number: 93-87704

ISBN: 0-7821-1495-4

Manufactured in the United States of America

10 9 8 7 6 5 4 3 2 1

This book is dedicated to the Ottawa Bunch—Julie Dustin, Laura Dexter, and John McFettridge (and Chris, of course). They've made Ottawa one of my favorite towns.

After having done this book, I have a lot more respect for the GUI interface designers at Microsoft and Apple. I have borrowed many ideas from their publications and their products; I thank them for that. Those guys did the hard work; I'm just reporting where they've been.

Christa Anderson had a tremendous amount to do with the writing of this, and indeed she wrote some of it. The controls chapter is largely her work, and good work it is.

Donna Cook sold the class that this book came from and Gerry Ross was the client that asked for it; thanks to both of them. As with all of my SYBEX books, this wouldn't have happened without the assistance of SYBEX's Maxwell Perkins, Gary Masters. And I'd never have gotten hooked up with SYBEX without the relentless bush-beating of my agent, Jeff Herman.

CONTENTS AT A GLANCE

CHAPTER *3*

USING WINDOWS IN A GUI APPLICATION

CHAPTER *4*

MAKING INPUT EASY

CHAPTER 5

CHAPTER 8

DESIGNING DIALOG BOXES THAT SPEAK CLEARLY 117

*D*eveloping applications in graphical environments was unheard-of just a few years ago. The growth of popularity in graphical environments like UNIX's X Windows, OS/2's Workplace Shell, the Macintosh, and of course Microsoft Windows, coupled with the drives to downsize applications from mainframes and convert successful DOS applications to newer operating systems, have forced many programmers to move from the familiar fields of structured design and structured programming to the less-familiar field of interfaced design.

Once, graphical user interface (GUI) programming was solely the province of those few C-programming stalwarts who braved mountains of bad documentation, studying for days before managing to get that first "Hello, world!" program to stagger to its feet. Nowadays, visual programming tools like Visual Basic and Powerbuilder in the Windows world, Hypercard in the Macintosh world, and VX-REXX under OS/2 2.1 enable you to build your first GUI program in minutes. You can actually design and build a small, useful program in a few hours.

That's good news for the mainframe programmer who's got to learn something besides COBOL and CICS if she wants to keep her job. It's good news for the support person accustomed to banging out the odd QBASIC ditty to solve some small problem. And it's good news for the after-hours hobbyist who likes to slap together a utility or game now and then, and who needs something a bit easier to work with than C and the Software Development Kit (SDK)—but that still creates Windows-compatible code.

Unfortunately, however, it's often *bad* news for the users of those programs. Turning a programmer loose with a plethora of buttons, scroll bars, windows, and menus often leads to a program that contains not a *graphical* user interface, but a *grotesque* user interface.

Believe me, I *know* about this. The first Windows programs that I turned out with Visual Basic did the job but were downright ugly. What's worse, I *knew* that they were ugly, but I had no idea what to do about it. Even worse, the people who used my programs knew that they were ugly.

Ever heard the old saw that goes, "I don't know art... but I know what I like"? It's the same thing with a well-designed GUI program. Your users may not be expert GUI designers, they may not be able to tell you exactly *what* is wrong, but they'll know that something *is* wrong. Hours of twiddling may make things better, but not necessarily.

Now, I looked around for some guidance on GUI design, and didn't find much—I was using Visual Basic version 1.0, and it was pretty new for *everyone*. Since then, I've used GUI programming tools on the Mac and OS/2 2.0/2.1, and time—as well as some very useful references—has allowed me to assemble some rules for building attractive GUI programs. That's why I wrote this book. Just as writers need style guides, like Strunk and White's *Elements of Style*, GUI programmers need a style guide. The things in this guide are drawn from a number of sources, and some of what's in here is just simple common sense. But it's intended to inspire you and to simplify the task of making good GUI programs. My examples are drawn largely from the Windows world, and for Visual Basic, as that's the tool that I use the most. But the ideas apply in any modern GUI.

This is not a book of absolute answers. No style guide is. It's a starting point for designers. So when you're in doubt, take a look in here for a suggestion. Throughout this book, remember two rules:

> **Rule 1: You're trying to build a GUI program that won't get noticed.** When I say that, what I mean is that the GUI interface should have all the basic elements in place, and in their proper places. The "help" menu item shouldn't pull *up* from the bottom of the window, the buttons should be gray, and the fonts should be the standard system fonts. People should notice what your program *does*, rather than how it presents itself. Let me draw an analogy from public speaking: If I do a keynote speech at a conference, then I will (I hope) say some informative and interesting things; I want to be remembered for that. I *don't* want to be remembered as the guy who stood up and spoke while wearing that interesting purple jacket and yellow ascot.
>
> **Rule 2:** If some rule doesn't fit, or doesn't make sense, then remember: **A good designer knows when to break the rules.** Just make sure you know exactly *what* the rule is, and *why* you're breaking that rule.

GUI design and GUI programming form an art that didn't even *exist*, in a practical sense, just ten years ago. You and I and everyone programming for GUIs today are part of a process of definition. The marketplace is evolving what I think of as "the new grammar," a grammar of visual elements in GUIs, movies, art, and television. As children, we used Strunk and White's landmark gem *The Elements of Style* as a guide to good writing. While I'm not anywhere near as good as Strunk and White, I thought much about them as I wrote this book. I sincerely hope that you will turn to this volume one-tenth as often as I've turned to *Elements of Style*. Use this book, and build something *beautiful!*

CHAPTER 1

A

PHILOSOPHY

OF

GOOD

DESIGN

*L*et's start off from the top: why bother with all the fuss of GUI programming, anyway?

Well, in a word: because it's what people *want*. And I can prove it. You can pick up a 386SX-based computer for just a few hundred dollars … but no one does. 486es and faster computers are the order of the day. But think about it. Remember 1989, when WordPerfect version 5.1 and 1-2-3 version 2.2 were major applications? Programs like that ran wonderfully on a 16-MHz 386SX with four megabytes of RAM. Moving to Windows versions of those packages means moving to 33-MHz computers with eight to 16 megabytes of memory and hundreds of megabytes of hard disk space…and yet people do it. It's not too outrageous to say that *the only reason that 486s and faster 386s exist is to support Windows.* That means that a *lot* of people are spending a *lot* of money, just to "go GUI." So the answer to "why bother?" is "because your customers—your users—want GUI."

So, if you're going to build a GUI application, it's worthwhile to look at what a GUI environment is supposed to do, and what it *can* do. That's what this first chapter is about: a look at some overall philosophy, before we dig into the nuts and bolts of the remaining chapters.

There's no one "right" way to build a GUI or a GUI application. But there are a number of guiding principles that should remain close to mind for GUI developers. GUI programs should have these characteristics:

They work with the user. A good GUI application behaves in a DWIM (Do What I Mean) manner. This means that the application lets the user arrange her desktop how she likes (for example, not insisting that the toolbox be in one spot on the screen), and can anticipate what she might do next based on what you've already been doing. The application's memory shouldn't be *too* good, however: If the user makes a mistake and must exit and reenter the program, the application should not return her to the same point at which she left and repeat the error.

GUI programs should be predictable. There are two parts to this characteristic: predictability based on world experience, and predictability based on other GUI applications.

In a graphical environment, we expect to see things as we encounter them in the real world: A drawing tool could look like a pencil, a zoom tool could look like a magnifying glass, and so on. The point of working in a graphical environment is lost if you have to work to identify your tools; for example, if the zoom tool looks like a Z or, worse, a badly-drawn microscope icon.

A good GUI design recognizes how people see things in the real world, but a good design also recognizes that other applications are part of that world. We've become accustomed to seeing a fill tool represented as a roller brush, for example. Since that's true, it's helpful if *all* applications that have fill tools represent them as roller brushes rather than something else; even if that something else might make more sense than the roller brush, the new element would force users to work harder to learn the application. A good GUI application builds on the success of others, behaving consistently so that the user doesn't have to relearn everything every time that he learns a new application. Once you've learned one GUI application, you should be able to use others pretty easily.

GUIs are sometimes claimed to be "intuitive." No matter what anybody says, user interfaces are *not* intuitive. There's nothing intuitive about double-clicking. What people mean when they say that GUIs are "intuitive" is that once someone explains a GUI to you, then you can take an application that you've never used before and *intuit* what it'll probably do under new circumstances. And, if the GUI is indeed intuitive, then your intuited guess will be correct. Or, as I've sometimes put it in class, "GUIs are intuitive, once someone explains them to you."

Attractive. If you make your GUI application pleasant to look at, people will be more liable to use it. Pay attention to control spacing, text size and other aesthetic issues. (Refer to Chapter 9, *Understanding and Using Controls* for more information.)

Easy to read. This is related to the attractiveness issue: If your application's dialog boxes and help files are easy to read, they're more attractive. Avoid jargon and strange typefaces. While strange fonts may satisfy your creative urges, they'll make your text harder to read and absorb. Don't experiment with different ways to arrange the OK and Cancel buttons. Stay with the things that people have become used to—even if you think they're not very good, or "intuitive."

Independent of monitor type and resolution. A good GUI application is useful on a variety of output devices, running equally well on 640×480 and 1024×768 screens.

Also, more and more people are working from laptops these days: You can't afford to ignore LCD screens. Some tools are better than others for this. It's relatively simple in Visual Basic to adjust your windows according to resolution. In FoxPro for Windows, in contrast, there is (believe it or not—after all, Microsoft makes FoxPro) no recognition of the need to support multiple resolutions and, according to a Microsoft spokesperson, no intention at all to add that support. (I guess the moral of the story is that you should choose your GUI development tools carefully.)

Customizable. Since different people have different working habits, you can't design an application for everyone's benefit. Therefore, your applications should be flexible in aesthetics (such as color) and structure (such as arrangement of menus). Don't expect the user to do all the work, however—plan some good defaults that give him somewhere to start from.

A good GUI will force UI consistency. In theory (and as I hinted earlier), it imposes consistency on a user interface (this is not GUI-specific, but rather UI-specific).

Non-distracting. While you want your GUI application to be pleasant to look at, it should also be invisible. The point of any application is not to open dialog boxes, press control buttons or read menus; the point is to get work done. Your goal as a GUI designer should be to make people more productive, not to create an exciting application. Cute File Open dialog boxes that parade file names past with cleverly chosen icons can be the source of *ooohs* and *ahhhs* the first time, but become indescribably annoying after the third.

Application integration. A good GUI application should be able to support a number of different kinds of files— allowing you, for example, to insert pictures into a text file.

Offer object orientation (drag 'n' drop). A graphical environment is based on objects, not text. As such, a user should be able to perform all or most commands with the mouse (or with keyboard hotkeys), rather than with typed commands. For example, users should be able to move most objects by dragging them with the mouse, rather than by typing the coordinates of the location where they want the object to be. On the other hand, the direct-entry approach is valuable too, and may lend itself to a DDE or OLE macro language.

Avoid copyright infringements. Building your application with a standard GUI should solve (or reduce) the "look and feel" legal question.

Forgiveness. Most people learn best through experimentation, playing with different buttons until they've got an idea of how they work. Therefore, you (as the GUI application designer) need to make it possible for your future users to back out of any corners they trap themselves in, whether through mispointing and selecting the wrong option or through not being sure which option to use. Your application should be able to handle errors well: providing ways to back out of dialog boxes or menus; minimizing the possiblity for error by providing clear options; and, when necessary, displaying clear and non-accusative error messages.

Getting to DWIM (Do What I Mean)

One of the whole reasons why GUIs appeared in the first place is so that user interfaces could become more "object oriented;" that is, so that you'd see something that metaphorically resembled a desktop, with objects on it that you could move around almost like *real* objects.

That's a worthy goal, but it doesn't stop there. You arrange things on your desk, and in your filing cabinet, so that they are *where* you want them, *when* you want them. How would you like your desk randomly rearranged every time that you use it, or a desk that refused to leave anything where you put it, insisting instead that the stapler *must* sit on the near right-hand corner? That's how many GUIs behave.

Anticipate Actions

The best possible behavior for any interactive program would be to anticipate your next move, and offer it as an alternative. Here are some examples.

- List boxes that remember where you last took an input from, so that it's not necessary to backtrack every time you open a document.

- Telescoping input fields: Press **A**, and everything disappears but the options that begin with *A*. Then press **R**, and everything disappears but the options that begin with *AR*, and so on.

- Present data to the user in the order in which she *uses* it, not some arbitrary order.

Provide Escape Hatches

Note, however, that there should always be an "escape hatch" in your program; if I do something dumb when I run the program and crash it *once*, then I don't want it to repeat the action automatically the next time that I start the program up.

The Next Best Thing: Predictability

If you can't read *my* mind, at least make it possible for me to read *yours*. If I'm running some goofy program that always puts the "Cancel" key in the wrong place, like the one in Figure 1.1, I could be in a lot of trouble.

FIGURE 1.1

A misarranged dialog box

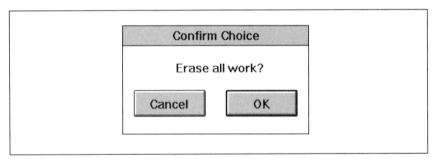

Now, this is a dumb dialog box because, first, the default action is fairly dangerous—pressing ↵ will get you an "OK," which will erase important work—and second, the OK button is on the right when it should be on the left.

But suppose I've been working with this program for a while, and I've gotten used to its idiosyncrasies. *Then* suppose I pull up some function that I've never used before, and get another OK/Cancel box ... but *this* time, the OK and Cancel are in the right places. I may well click the wrong button because I won't look closely at the buttons.

GUI Programs Should Be Attractive

If you ever used a Windows 1 or 2 application, then you may recognize the buttons shown in Figure 1.2.

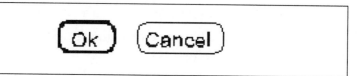

Those are the buttons used in older version of Windows. They do the exact same thing as the buttons shown in Figure 1.3.

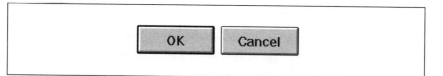

What's the real difference between these two sets of buttons, anyway? After all, both express the same characters, right?

Kind of, yes; but not really. The second set of buttons has a "3-D" feel to it. The introduction of the 3-D controls in Windows 3.x gave that GUI a more "professional" feel. Additionally, look at the Windows 3 colors when compared to the Windows 1 or 2 colors. The first time Windows 3.0 popped that "Windows" logo up on my screen, I saw a shade of blue that I didn't even know my VGA could *display*! It generated a kind of excitement that I didn't expect from a graphical user interface; your programs can generate that same kind of excitement ... do they?

GUI Programs Should Be Easy to Read

Screens are harder to read than paper. Therefore, you've got to be easy on your users:

Use a standard font: Choose fonts carefully. Dialog boxes are not the arena in which to experiment with fonts.

Choose color with care: Select foreground and background colors so that they complement each other. Also, make sure that there's enough difference between active and dimmed options that the user doesn't have to waste time clicking inactive options—valid choices should be obvious.

Be flexible about color: Test color sets in applications against different Windows color schemes, just to make sure that you're not dependent on your user using a particular color combination.

Don't tailor it to one monitor type: Check text screens on LCD screens—monochrome vs. color, and active matrix vs. passive matrix.

GUI Programs Must Be Useful on a Variety of Output Devices

Too many developers see screens like LCD screens as an unimportant side-issue. That's crazy; look at most Apple Power-Books or the Hewlett-Packard "instant-on" Windows three-pound portable for classic examples of LCD machines whose sole purpose in life is to support GUIs.

• More and more Windows programs seem to have been built for 1024 × 768 screens, and look horrible under VGA and unreadable under monochrome LCD.

- GUI programs must be as resolution-independent as possible. We'll talk more later about making sure your applications work under a variety of resolutions.

GUI Programs Must Be Customizable

Even if there is an aspect of *your* particular GUI implementation that rubs users the wrong way, letting them make their own changes to parts of the environment makes it more comfortable. For example, a major change under Windows 3.1 was the ability to play with colors, bitmaps, and icons—all essentially useless doodads that often translate into excuses to waste time; but people *like* customizing. Just look at any workstation cubicle, and you'll see tacked-up pictures of kids, spouses … you get the idea. Allowing a user to put his "mark" on your application makes him more likely to "adopt" it as his own.

Customizability refers to non-GUI things as well: Default directories and equipment environment are two examples.

GUI Programs Must Be Forgiving

How do I tell the dialog box shown in Figure 1.4, "forget it"?

Give up? The answer is "Close" … I think. There should be a clear escape hatch, as I said earlier. And the answer isn't simply to put a Cancel button on every dialog box—although that *should* be part of your programming gospel; and the Cancel button should be in a consistent place.

FIGURE 1.4

A dialog box that seems to lack an exit

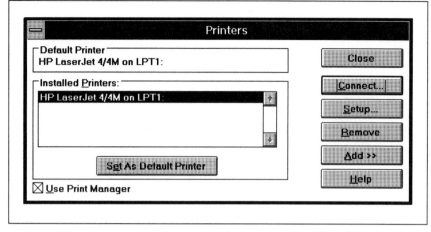

GUI Programs Should Make People More Productive

Dragging and dropping is quicker than figuring out which input filter will be required to pull in a DXF file. GUIs also should make it easy to:

- *See* what a program can do, through the menu, and
- *Try out* features without fear (forgiveness, remember).

Also, an application should allow a user to perform her tasks efficiently, without spending too much time thinking about the application itself.

GUIs Should Allow Application Integration

Cut and paste, DDE and OLE, Apple Events, Publish and Subscribe are all examples of methods whereby GUIs allow users to leverage good programs.

That's "good" programs because so many program authors don't employ the full benefit of things like the Clipboard in Windows. Yes, DDE and OLE programming is challenging and, worse, flaky.

Good application integration means that programs should be integrated into the Windows environment in that they should be able to respond to a wide variety of files—file types including these:

TEXT FILES	GRAPHICS FILES	OTHER FILES
ASCII	PCX	Sound (WAV)
RTF	Windows BMP	Video (AVI)
Word Perfect 5.x	Windows Metafiles (WMF)	
WordStar	AutoCAD DXF	
Word for DOS	Computer Graphics Metafile (CGM)	
Ami Pro	TIFF	
SGML	EPS	
Excel spreadsheets		
123 spreadsheets		
dBase databases		

TEXT FILES	GRAPHICS FILES	OTHER FILES
Windows Write		
Word for Windows		

You can't support all of those formats … or can you? With OLE servers, it is more and more possible to buy "plug in" file format compatibility.

GUI Environments Solve (or Reduce) the "Look and Feel" Legal Question

Sad, but true: there's some real value to having someone *else* (someone large and in the northwestern US) worry about whether or not you're violating some ancient patent. Lotus and Borland slugged it out for years about whether or not Borland stepped on Lotus's territory when it added a 1-2-3–like user interface to Quattro Pro for Windows. (They did, according to the court, and Borland suffered a wound from which it may not recover.) Similarly, Microsoft and Apple spent years in court deciding whether or not Windows looks too much like the Mac. (It doesn't, according to the court.) Any Windows programmer or Mac programmer has those worries essentially removed by the fact that the interface is *Microsoft's* problem, not theirs.

The Tough Question: Are GUIs Consistent?

Are *your* applications as "consistent" as the dialog boxes shown in Figure 1.5? There are common dialog boxes (covered later) that make consistency easier. But a good, consistent scheme for building dialogs is more important than giving in

FIGURE 1.5

Example of various "File Open" dialog boxes

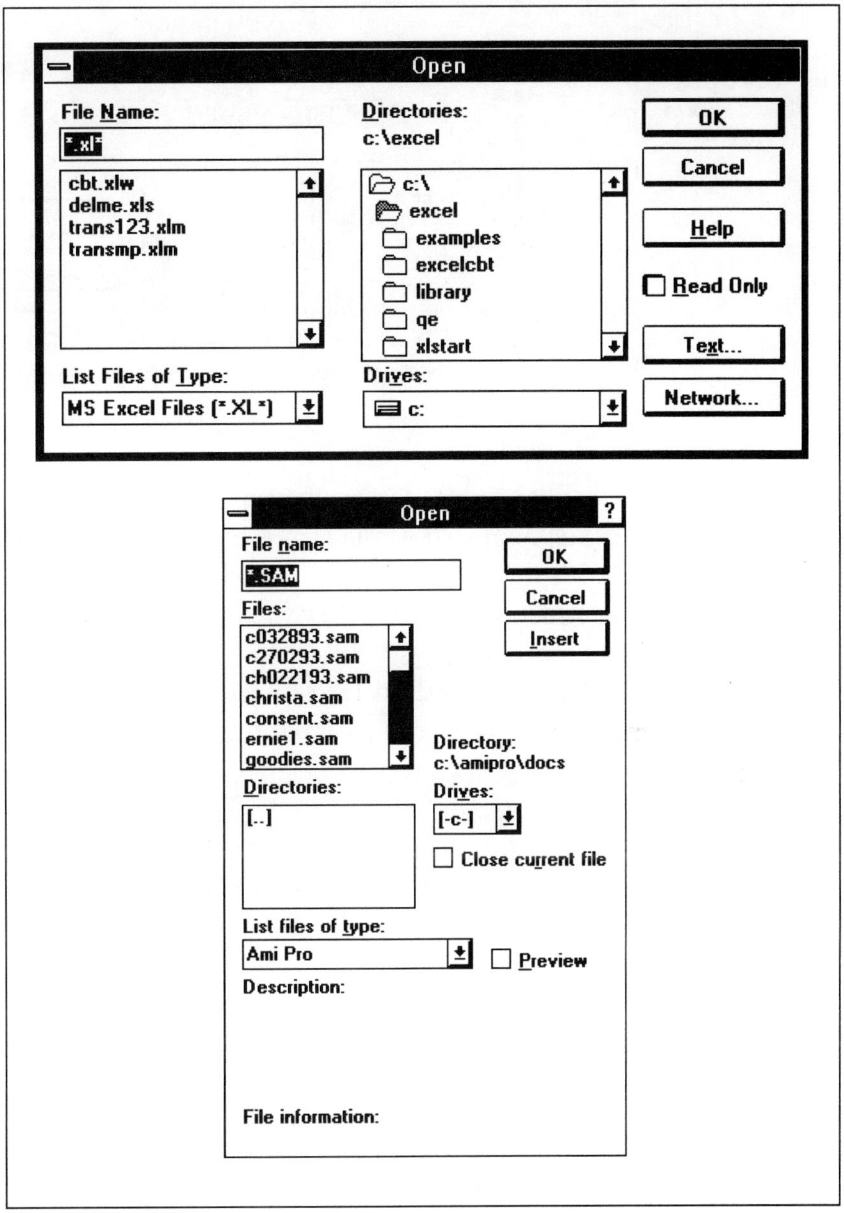

FIGURE 1.5

Example of various "File Open" dialog boxes (continued)

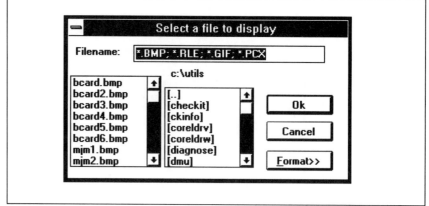

to brilliant ideas later, when the project is halfway done. "A needless consistency is the hobgoblin of small minds," certainly—but there's nothing needless about making life easier for your users.

CHAPTER 2

GUI

ELEMENTS

O ne of the most annoying parts of GUI development is all the new terminology. You probably know what a title bar is, but do you know the difference between a combo box and list box?

This chapter introduces the parts of the Windows GUI, as it is the most widespread GUI.

Windows

The central element of Windows' GUI is, of course, the windows themselves.

Application windows: These make up the basic visual framework for data and commands in an application—they're what you see when you open an application. Most action in an application takes place in an application window.

Multiple Document Interface (MDI) windows: This type of window allows the application to handle more than one document (or more than one copy of the same document) at a time. Only one window of this type is active at a time.

Help windows: These are actually independent application windows, and can be moved outside the primary application window.

Dialog boxes: Some application commands require more information than one keystroke can give. When this is the case, pressing such a command produces a dialog box that prompts the user for more information and contains controls that let the user supply it.

Icons, Bitmaps, and Drawings

GUIs intend for a picture to tell a thousand words—although bad icons often require more than a thousand words to explain them.

Aldus Made Everyone a Publisher; Who Will Make Everyone a Rembrandt?

Normal word processing made it easy for anyone to produce nice, typewriter-like or printed-like output of English text. But writing is something that we're all trained to do from first grade through 12th grade. GUIs, in contrast, rely heavily upon *pictures*—and most of us have little talent for drawing.

That means that developers must be careful when planning for diagrams. A recent study by Westinghouse showed that:

- presentations are enhanced by good graphics, but

- presentations are *harmed* by bad graphics

Bad graphics are worse than no graphics at all. Icon libraries and clip art can help here. Or break down and hire the services of a graphics designer; they're not that expensive, and they're cheaper than bankruptcy from lousy sales.

Be Careful of Copyrights!

It's tempting to grab that scene from a movie or television show, or use some GIF file in your application. But before you do, make sure that you've got the copyrights cleared. Copyright violations make for very expensive lawsuits. As I mentioned in the last chapter, Apple and Microsoft sued each other for *years* over copyright infringement.

And if you think that some of this is a bit picayune, consider this: In the final year of the Apple–Microsoft suit, the judge had thrown out everything about the case *except* the question of whether or not Microsoft infringed Apple's rights by using the *trash can icon*! Clever artistic expression is protected by law—don't run afoul of it.

Drawings vs. Bitmaps

Within the GUI universe, there are two ways of storing and building pictures:

- as bitmaps, also known as *rasters*, or
- as drawings, also known as *vector* or *object diagrams*

The difference is simple but important. With a bitmap, a picture is stored as a collection of dots—*pixels* or *pels*—that can be shown on the screen or the printer. Drawings are stored as a series of objects, instructions on how to draw a picture.

For example, if you use a bitmap-creation program like Paintbrush and you tell Paintbrush to put a circle on the screen, then Paintbrush computes which dots are part of a circle, and then changes the colors of those dots on the screen. Once you've moved on to your next task, however, then Paintbrush *forgets* that those dots are a circle; you can't go back to Paintbrush and say, "resize this circle" or "repaint this circle". Paintbrush doesn't know a circle *is*, except to paint it.

In contrast, a drawing program like CorelDRAW! or Designer remembers what the components of each diagram are, and stores the file not as how the picture looks, but as how the picture should be created: There is an internal representation of each drawing command. Where a bitmap file would look like "Green dot, green dot, white dot, blue dot, green dot...," a drawing file would look like "Draw a blue circle with radius 15 around center coordinate (15,15)."

Both bitmaps and drawing files have their place in the GUI world. Bitmaps are larger files, and they are resolution dependent, but they can be fine-tuned and anti-aliased (a process that you'll learn about in Chapter 5 that smooths the look of a bitmap), things that are harder with drawings. The small size of icons *requires* that they be bitmaps. Drawings, on the other hand, are easier to store, resolution independent, and easier to revise, making them appropriate for things that will require revision and printing in different sizes—for example, technical drawings.

Examples of bitmap file formats in Windows are

- TIFF (Tagged Image File Format): Often scanned images are stored in TIFF.

- PCX (Paintbrush) is an old bitmap format that many bitmaps are distributed in.

- BMP is the Windows Bitmap format, adapted from a bitmap format developed by Microsoft for OS/2.

Common drawing file formats in Windows include:

- WMF (Windows Metafile), adapted from a picture format developed by Microsoft for OS/2.

- DXF, an AutoDesk format often used for exporting Auto-CAD files.

- CGM (Computer Graphics Metafile), used by Freelance and other packages.

- EPS (encapsulated PostScript), a vector language based on the PostScript printer-control language.

It's simple to go from drawing formats to bitmap formats, but not the other way around.

Menus

As I've already noted, menus are an essential part of what makes GUIs attractive. If all of a program's features are displayed on a menu, then there an incentive to look further into exactly what each of those features do.

Alternatively, some command-driven programs might require commands like:

```
list 20 30 when "abc" col 45 46 unnumbered
```

to get something done. That's an example of a very powerful command language called SuperWylbur. It's great, but it takes months to get really proficient with. If SuperWylbur had menus, then you could be productive with it in minutes instead of months.

Types Of Menus

In most windowed environments, you'll see:

- standard two-level menus
- cascaded menus (menus that branch from other menu items)
- tear-off menus (menus that can be moved to another screen location)

We'll discuss menus further in the Chapter 6, *Constructing Useful Menus*.

Message and Dialog Boxes

Windows programs can display other windows, small windows that either solicit or provide information. These windows are called *dialog boxes*. A dialog box that only provides information, offering only an OK button (for example, an error message), gets the more specific name *message box*. Message boxes are so common that they're often treated like something separate from dialog boxes, but they are indeed just a special form of dialog box.

Controls

The contents of dialog boxes are usually graphical items that provide alternatives for input. Simple input is accomplished with just buttons, but there are many other input option items; you see many of them—the input items are called *controls*—in Figure 2.1.

FIGURE 2.1

**A variety of controls
in a dialog box**

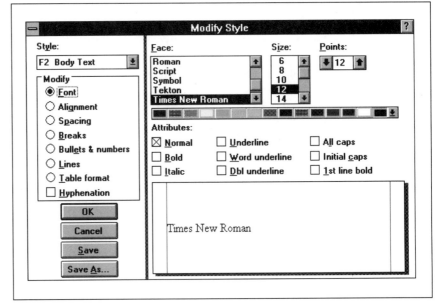

I turn again for examples to Ami Pro; this is the Modify Style dialog box. You see it if you either choose Styles ➤ Modify Style, or if you right-click a paragraph. Don't worry so much about what it does; instead, notice what it *contains*. In the upper-left corner, there's a *drop-down single-selection list box* that lets you choose the style to modify. Below that, there is a *group box*, a partial rectangle filled with *radio buttons* that let you specify which aspect of the style that you want to modify. *Check boxes* let you specify attributes; they're situated just below a *value set* that shows a range of possible colors, which in turn sits below two *single-selection list boxes* and a *combo box*. There is a sample showing what the style you've built will look like in the lower-right corner in a control called a *static text box*. The dissected version of this dialog box appears in Figure 2.2.

FIGURE 2.2

**A dissected
dialog box**

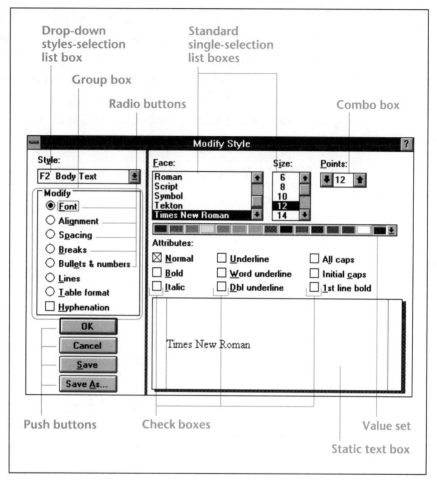

This doesn't even describe the full range of controls; you'll
meet all of them in Chapter 9, *Understanding and Using
Controls.*

Toolbars

Another post-3.1 feature that we see a lot of in Windows programs is toolbars, a strip of icons that activate menu items. It

has become *de rigeur*, but it's often not done well. In the next chapter, you'll see a screen shot from Ami Pro that shows the Lotus approach, SmartIcons. It uses 32 by 32 pixel colored icons to indicate what the icon does; you can alternatively click an icon with the right mouse button, and the title bar will explain what the icon does. This is a toolbar as it should be done.

Colors aren't *essential*; take for instance, the toolbar from Visual BASIC Professional Edition (Figure 2.3).

F I G U R E **2.3**

The Visual Basic Toolbar

It's easy to distinguish which tools produce picture objects, labels, text, radio buttons, and so on. That can't really be said for *all* Microsoft toolbars, however. Look at some of these icons taken from the Windows for Workgroups File Manager toolbar (Figure 2.4).

What do these icons do? The one with the *8* under the *7* is mutually exclusive with the one that looks like the boxes that get smaller and smaller.

If you don't know, you'll likely not guess that the 8/7 icon sorts files by date, and the boxes icon sorts files by size. The *a._* icon says to sort by file names; the *_.a* icon says to sort by extensions. Has the definite look of a last-minute job, doesn't it?

Moral of the story: Icons are terrific story-tellers, and a whole band of them can be wonderful. But they'd better be understandable, or they just take up valuable real estate.

New-Wave Feedback

It doesn't end with this introduction. I've recently seen Help files that say "Thank you for purchasing XYZ product"—and when I say "say," I mean *say*—right out of the speaker.

(These files are known as "wave" files because of their extension, WAV.) As is so often the case, it's games that are ahead of business applications *currently*; for instance, I sometimes play a shareware game called Card Shark Hearts that emits a satisfied "Cool!" when it shoots the moon, or a frustrated "Bogus!" when stuck with the Queen of Spades.

At minimum, many Windows programs make the default "beep" sound when you make a mistake, or when they want to announce an important message. Such generic sounds are fairly useless, and in time we'll see more and more programs that employ a variety of sounds.

If you *do* use sounds, however, be sure to keep them simple. Words may not be distinguishable when spoken through the speaker of a desktop PC. Musical tones, however, can usually be understood.

Beyond sounds, there are now AVI (Audio/Video Interleaved) files that contain full-motion videos within themselves. It is possible to embed one of those files into a Help system, but at a price that is, today, too high: tens of megabytes just for a few minutes of video. As CD-ROM–based products become more widespread, that too will change, and for sound as well as video. Extensive sound libraries can take up tons of storage space.

USING

WINDOWS

IN

A

GUI

APPLICATION

W hile this seems a bit recursive—"Why would you use windows in Windows?"—there are a few mechanicals that you should understand before plotting out a Windows program.

Since Windows 3.1, a lot of new capabilities have been built into windows and windowing. This is, then, an overview of windowing possibilities.

Window Types

I discussed these in the last chapter, but let's review:

- *Application windows* or *main program* windows are the normal window, the "default" window.

- *Document*, *Child*, or *MDI* (Multiple Document Interface) windows are windows that live entirely inside other windows.

- *Help* windows are independent windows that can move outside of the application window (because they're largely driven not by the application but instead by the Windows Help Engine, which is itself the program WINHELP.EXE.

- *Dialog boxes* are semi-independent windows generated by the same application that raised the original window.

Parts of a Window

Windows programs can have three possible states:

- **Minimized,** which shows just an icon
- **Maximized,** which fills the screen
- **Windowed,** where the program only fills up part of the screen

A normal Windows program may look like Figure 3.1 when windowed.

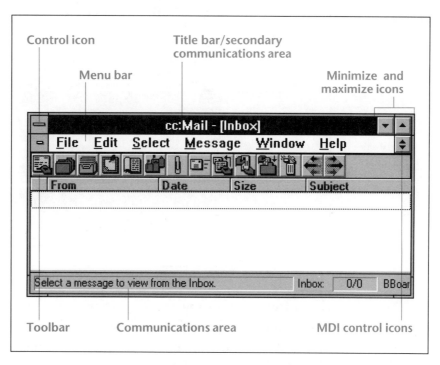

Most of the items are self-explanatory, but there are a few items worth commenting on.

The Communications/Status Area

The *Communications area*, *status line*, or *message bar* is something that's become popular since Windows 3.1 appeared. Messages appear in a recessed gray area on the bottom of the window in black text. The messages are either suggestions about what to do next, as you see in the cc:Mail window shown in Figure 3.1, or they can provide information about what's under the mouse, as you see in the window shown in Figure 3.2.

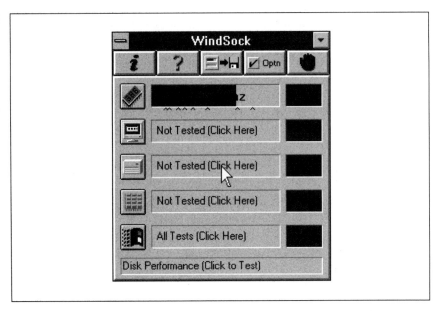

What I want you to notice in particular is that the cursor sits over some text that refers to a disk benchmark test (that's the icon to the left of the text), and the communication area says *Disk Performance (Click to Test)*. I don't have to *click* anything to get this; merely passing the mouse pointer over the area gets the information.

Communications Area Problems

I'm not 100 percent sure that this is a feature that everyone should include in their Windows applications; I used this program for *months* before noticing that anything happens in the communications area when the cursor floats over a window button.

To an extent, this is related to a design problem in the communications area. The communications area also lacks (in my opinion *solely*—this is a point that you will not find everyone echoing) in that it shows black text against a light gray background. It doesn't call out to me; even if it said *Warning: You'll trash your computer if you do this. Do you want to continue?*, I might not even notice that it was there.

Using the Title Bar
as a Secondary Communications Area

Some programs, Ami Pro and the other Lotus offerings in particular, use the title bar as a communications area, as you see in Figure 3.3.

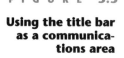

F I G U R E 3.3

Using the title bar as a communica-tions area

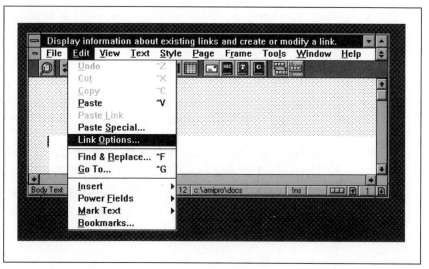

Notice here that the Edit menu is selected for the Link Options… item, and the title bar says *Display information about existing links and create or modify a link*. Now, *this* is a useful place to put a communications area; it's got good contrast—bright white against a dark background—and it appears up at the top of a window, where your eye is more likely to notice it.

Split Windows

Some applications must show two separate parts of a window in the same area; as a result, they divide the top from the bottom with a *split bar*.

Panes within Split Windows

The window is then divided into *panes*, each of which may have a scroll bar. Within the panes, the user can examine two parts of a document (such as a spreadsheet) at the same time, or two views (such as an outline view and a text view). All panes should lie within the parameters of the main window.

Synchronized Scrolling

Multipane windows may require an option for synchronized scrolling, so as to make it easier for the user to compare a document's views. Windows does not provide any programming help for this, so if you need it, you'll have to do it by hand.

If you *do* want to offer synchronized scrolling (and you really should—look at the Windows Setup's display of the AUTO-EXEC.BAT/CONFIG.SYS "before installation" and "after installation" for an example of how to do it right), then you should offer the option to disable it as well.

Resizing Windows

Windows by default provides support for window resizing. However, in many windows—dialog boxes in particular—that may not be desirable. For example, consider the seemingly innocent dialog box shown in Figure 3.4.

FIGURE 3.4

**An adjustable
dialog box**

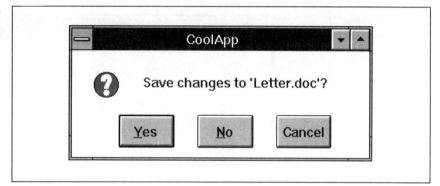

It *looks* pretty normal, but look more closely: There's a minimize and maximize icon on the window, and there are *resizing borders* on the window! A user might accidentally end up changing the dialog box, making it look like Figure 3.5 and possibly not realizing that there's a Cancel option offered.

FIGURE 3.5

**The adjustable
dialog box after
resizing**

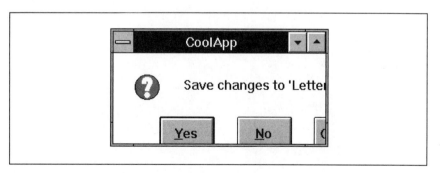

Worse yet, one of your competitors might do this on purpose, take a screen shot of it, and send it to *Windows* magazine, where you'd be publicly embarrassed; *seppuku* would be the only honorable option at that point. Instead, consider the dialog box shown in Figure 3.6.

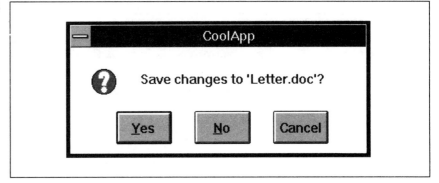

Same information, but *this* time there'll be no drolleries from the beta testers.

CHAPTER 4

MAKING

INPUT

EASY

GUI interfaces have made much of mice as pointing devices, so much in fact that many GUI programs seem to focus only on the mouse. But keyboards are equally important to getting information into your system and getting work done—perhaps more important than mice when all's said and done.

Comparing Input Devices

What I *really* want is a direct neural tap…

Types of Input

There are three kinds of input:

- **Pointing:** directing a program's attention to a particular object or option. You do this when you initiate an action through a menu, or when responding to a program query in a dialog box.

- **Selection:** choosing an item or a range of items. You do this in a list box, for example.

- **Data entry:** entering text and numbers. This is, of course, how the majority of the data in the computer world originates.

Both mice and keyboards have strengths and weaknesses in these areas.

Mouse Strengths and Weaknesses

The mouse is first a *pointing* device, second a *selection* device, and third a data-entry device. (Really: Consider the Calculator, where you can enter numbers by clicking on them—that's data entry.)

Most of a mouse's strengths are related to its agility in moving across the screen:

- Mice are extremely good for pointing.

- They're even better with "ballistic" mouse support (the mouse starts out moving slowly but then accelerates as you keep moving it), which Windows doesn't usually provide but which you can build in.

- Don't build ballistic support into your *application*, however: If you do, your application will feel different from other Windows apps, and that's bad. But if you can offer ballistic Windows mouse drivers, then you improve the entire environment.

- Mice are excellent for single-item selection, but not as good for multiple-item selection (except in combination with the keyboard).

The mouse's weaknesses are:

- Mice are inadequate for selecting multipage data.

- Mice require more physical maintenance than do keyboards, and a malfunctioning mouse can be an incredible productivity-drainer.

- Mice can be inappropriate for portable computers, but this is becoming less of a problem as, thankfully, mouse analogs (trackballs, mini-joysticks) are filling that gap.

Keyboard Strengths and Weaknesses

A keyboard's strengths are based on its speed and familiarity:

- A keyboard offers a wider variety of possible inputs; not only are there dozens of keys, they can be modified by Ctrl, Alt, and Shift.

- A keyboard is a familiar input device—even people who have never touched a computer before probably have some typewriter experience, whereas experienced computer users are not necessarily mouse-literate.

- With training (touch typing), a keyboard can be a high-speed input device, as the user never needs to remove his hands from the keyboard to activate commands.

- A keyboard is an excellent device for large-scale selection (e.g., to select an entire 100-page document, press Ctrl-Home, then Shift-Ctrl-End; or in a growing number of applications, simply press Ctrl-A. The same process with a mouse requires scrolling through the entire hundred pages while holding down the button, and if you accidentally click before you're through you have to start over again).

A keyboard's weaknesses are:

- Keyboards may be off-putting to some sectors of the workplace—some people don't like using commands and prefer to point with the mouse. Some folks view keyboarding as degrading, the work of menials. (Fortunately, those people are disappearing.)

- The keyboard is largely inadequate for pointing unless the keyboard repeat rate is accelerated.

- The keyboard can't be used as a drawing tool.

Input Functions

There are several different kinds of input tools and modalities.

Pointing

You point, as you know, by moving the mouse, which causes the device driver and hardware kernel to move a small bitmap called the *cursor* around the screen.

Unmodified (i.e., no Shift, Ctrl, or Alt keys pressed) pointing should be a *passive* activity. Pointing at something shouldn't make something happen, with the one possible exception that status information might appear in the status/communication area.

I would *strongly* suggest against building in the "balloon help" that some programs use whereby if you move the cursor over something, then a balloon pops up explaining what that thing does. It's cute for about 30 seconds, but after that it wears a bit thin. Macintosh System 7 includes balloon help. Ever notice that no one uses it? It's so annoying that it gets turned off within an hour on most people's machines.

Clicking

The primary mouse function in GUIs is in selecting single items.

Left Mouse Button

Your applications should let users select things with the left mouse button (in Windows—it varies in other OSs) clicks.

Right Mouse Button

What about that *other* mouse button? What should it do? (Let's not even talk about the middle mouse button on the three-button mice.) There is no standard, but there've been some interesting uses from different vendors:

- Micrografx Designer allows you to use the right mouse button to adjust the position of a drawn object as you are drawing it; it's an essential feature that makes it possible to build really good diagrams.

- The latest suite of Microsoft applications uses the right button to pop up a menu (a "pop-up menu" or "floating menu," to be specific) with the basic editing commands on it.

- Ami Pro's right click brings up the dialog box that allows you to modify a paragraph style, which is kind of useful, but not *that* useful.

- Some image-processing programs bring up common dialogs like brightness/contrast with the right button.

- Some programs let you assign almost any function to the right mouse key.

Be creative and find a use for that extra button!

Dragging

One of the first techniques that any new GUI user must master is clicking and dragging. Once you know how to do it, it's simple; but remember that it's not as intuitive as people make it out to be, before enlightenment sets in. Clicks and drags are used for:

- multiple selection of text, lists, or cells

- moving of objects

- "rubberbanding" of areas on bitmaps or drawings for selection. As the user clicks and drags, a rectangle appears on screen. The rectangle's major diagonal runs from the point of the first click to the current cursor drag point.

Be Sure to Separate Selection and Moving

Inasmuch as selection and moving are two different actions, you should make clear which action the user is taking. Many Windows programs don't do that well. Take, for example, the Program Manager. Icons are objects, so clicking and dragging on an icon should move it. But double-clicking on an icon starts up the program associated with that icon. So people often find that when they double-click on an icon, Windows does not initially understand that the action is a double-click rather than a single-click, and so the icon gets moved askew before the application starts. Result: a messy program group in Program Manager.

Providing Clues to Drag Modes

You can indicate whether you're selecting or moving something by one of these methods:

Change the cursor shape. This is not recommended in general, but when you're moving or copying an object, then this is one of the times that you *should* change the cursor shape.

Outline it. Outline the object in some way.

Change the object's appearance. Change the look of the object in some way—outline it, reverse its color, or make it monochrome—to indicate that it is selected. Pushbuttons, for example, show that they are depressed by displaying a different bitmap when pushed, a bitmap providing the illusion that there actually *is* a slightly raised button on the screen. Some controls invert their colors when selected; this doesn't look like a real-world pushable item, but it confirms that the item has been selected.

You see another example in the Program Manager, which indicates that an icon is selected by highlighting its title. Perhaps as multimedia becomes more widespread, we'll see programs using a "click" sound or the like when buttons are depressed.

Ami Pro's Approach to Double Duty

Ami Pro tries to make the click/drag do double duty by letting you first select text, then drag that text somewhere. It often doesn't work, however, as the cursor is now *modal*—it behaves differently depending on whether or not there's text selected.

The *idea* is that you first click and drag across the text you want to move, then you release the mouse button and click again somewhere in the selected area. Keeping the mouse button down, you then drag the text to wherever you want it.

That's a nice feature, but it causes trouble when you have accidentally selected the wrong text. You'd like to go back and select a different set of text, so you click and drag again … but find that you're moving the old text. *Arrgh*.

I wish Windows would adopt the OS/2 approach: The left button selects, the right button moves and copies.

Double-Clicking

Double-clicking is typically used for quick action: Select and activate. But be aware of the following:

Double-clicking shouldn't be vital. Don't make it essential to the operation of the application; not everyone can double-click. And, no, I'm not kidding; it seems that about five percent of the GUI users—I have no solid statistics, I just base the five percent on my personal experience as an educator—find double-clicking as difficult as some folks find using chopsticks. (Call this *doubleclickslexia*, I suppose.) Again, it's supposed to be an application, not a video game.

Make double-clicking useful. Many programs have tons of "hidden features" behind their double clicks. Double-clicking the margins on one word processor makes Modify Page Format appear; double-clicking on a day on a scheduler makes details about the day appear, and the like. These things are conveniences—shortcuts—for simple tasks. People learn after a while that they can experiment with double-clicking to find shortcuts, and that double-clicking is *safe*. On that note ...

Keep double-clicking safe. What if double-clicking on a part of the Windows screen closed Windows and dropped all my open files without any confirmation? Heck, after *that* happened, I'd never double-click again. So make sure that double-clicking is risk-free.

Double-Dragging

This is pretty rare; it involves double-clicking, *then* dragging. I suggest that you avoid it, as it begins to make your program look less like an application and more like a video game.

Using Modifiers with the Mouse

Ctrl, Shift and Alt all modify the actions of the mouse. We'll discuss this more in the upcoming section on selection.

Use the Hourglass and Multitask Properly

This is a trifle off-topic, but as long as I'm talking about the mouse, be sure to change the cursor to an hourglass before commencing some operation that will take a while. For example, in Visual Basic, the code might look like:

```
mousepointer=11 'The hourglass
...lengthy calculation follows...
mousepointer=1 ' the normal pointer
```

This is considerate to the user, who needs to know that the computer isn't going to respond for a while.

And as long as I'm off-topic, let me take up an important item that doesn't really fit anywhere else into the book. In the Windows world, the multitasking of Windows programs is largely handled by the programs themselves. That means that it's very good practice to build the program so that it doesn't hog the CPU for extended periods of time (more than about 100 milliseconds). With Visual Basic, you'd do that by sprinkling calls to the DoEvents() function in your code, particularly in the middle of large looping data structures.

Mouse Input Tips

The mouse is the primary selection device in the GUI world. Subtle things like speed sensitivity on a mouse can radically affect the way that people perceive the responsiveness of your application. Here's a few things to keep in mind:

Use ballistic drivers if they exist. Once you've used a mouse for a while, you eventually come to see that on many systems, the mouse seems always to be too fast or too slow, too rough or too fine. For instance, when you want to whip the mouse across the screen, then you don't want to have to move it across your desk until you run out of space, then pick it up and move it to the other side of the desk, and then repeat the action; in this instance, the mouse seems too slow. In contrast, there are other times when you're trying to bit-fiddle some object on the screen, moving it over just a pixel or two. In that case, the mouse seems too fast and too coarse. A long time ago, Apple addressed that with their Mac mouse drivers. The Apple drivers were designed to be *speed sensitive*. Move the mouse quickly, and the mouse "takes big steps"—an inch of mouse movement on the desktop can translate to an entire screen's width of travel. Move it slowly, and it "takes baby steps"—that same inch of desk travel can translate into just a few pixel's movement. Not every GUI offers ballistic drivers (they're not present in most mouse drivers for Windows, for example), but if they're available, use them.

Don't be click-dependent. As I said a page or two back, don't make your application rely on double-clicking. Some people have trouble with it.

Gauge selection difficulty carefully. Consider how easy or hard it is to select an object, and adjust "hotspots" accordingly. If it's a text character or a spreadsheet cell, then merely pointing and clicking will be simple. But when clicking on an icon, must the pointer be exactly *on* the icon? Make the hotspots around small objects exceed the objects by a pixel or two. And remember that you can make *anything* a control, something that'll do some action if you click on it. How? Simple. To take a bitmap, say, of a company logo and make a message appear when the bitmap is clicked, just put a button on the same location as the bitmap, but *hide* the button. (In every GUI language I've worked with, you can put an invisible but active button on the screen in one of your program's windows.) Make the button a bit bigger than the bitmap, and it'll be easy to hit the bitmap and still get a response, even if you're a bit off.

Of course, if the action caused by clicking the object is important, then confirm the action—people aren't as sure that they're doing anything when they're clicking objects instead of menu items.

Don't mess with the cursor unnecessarily. Don't change the shape of the cursor unless you *must*; work mainly with the I-beam text pointer and the standard arrow pointer. This is important for two reasons: first, recognition—people "lock onto" the standard pointer more easily, as they recognize it; and second, it's often hard to see a cursor on a laptop screen, so laptop users employ utilities that can expand the standard pointer and the I-beam … but not other pointers. Another essential pointer adjustment, as I mentioned a few pages back, is the hourglass. If you're keeping the computer busy, then for heaven's sake *tell* the user.

Keyboard Input Modes

The keyboard's input modes in a GUI environment are the same as in a textual environment:

- Caps Lock enabled/disabled
- Num Lock enabled/disabled
- Ctrl depressed/released
- Alt depressed/released
- Shift depressed/released
- insert mode enabled/disabled
- Scroll Lock enabled/disabled

Some people include this information on their application's status line/communications area, as you see in Figure 4.1.

FIGURE 4.1

A screen displaying
toggle information

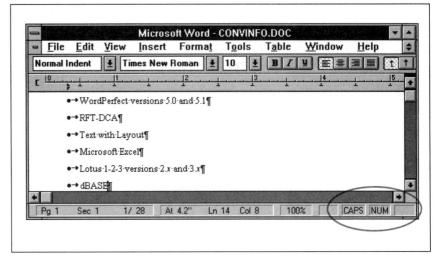

I'm not totally convinced of the necessity for the toggle information. If that's all that the status line is good for, then get rid of it and give the user back that space in which to view more spreadsheet rows or lines of text. At the least, let the user hide it and thus regain that space.

Mouse Backup Functions

Although most people aren't aware of it, you can perform many mouse functions with the keyboard. For example, you can resize, move, or close a window with the keyboard.

You don't have to worry about those particular keystrokes, as they come free with every window that you create (assuming that you hadn't gotten too far off the beaten track when you wrote your code), but bear in mind when building your systems that you should be able to do virtually anything with just the keyboard. There are three reasons for this:

- Sometimes the mouse ceases to work, or "freezes up." The keyboard can then be a backup input device that will allow your user to gracefully finish whatever she's doing, close up the application, and reset the system.

- Not all users *have* a mouse. Windows *says* that a mouse is required, but it will also run without a mouse.

- Fast keyboarders don't want to take their hands away from the keyboard, and want to do everything from the keyboard. You can use both the mouse and the keyboard, too. Really coordinated artists might use the keyboard to select items and the mouse to draw with.

GUIs are newer and flashier than CLIs, but there are more users of command line interfaces at present in the computer world than there are GUI users. Give people the chance to use the keyboard, and some of them will be more apt to use your application.

Shortcuts and Access Keys

Windows provides two ways to get to program capabilities from the keyboard: access keys and shortcut keys.

Access Keys

The keystrokes indicated by an underline, like *File*, are called *mnemonics* or *access keys*. You typically tell a Windows development tool to provide an access key by embedding an ampersand in the label. For example:

- a label **&File** would produce a menu item *File*

- a label **Save &As**... would produce a menu item
  Save As...

It only takes a minute to stick the ampersands in the references to keytop labels and menu items, so do it—your users will thank you. Make them unique—you don't want two Alt-F options.

Shortcut Keys/Accelerator Keys

Shortcut keys or *accelerator* keys are the keystrokes that let you directly access a function even if that function would otherwise require burrowing through several levels of menus. You can see shortcut keys in Figure 4.2.

F I G U R E **4.2**

Keyboard shortcut keys indicated on a menu

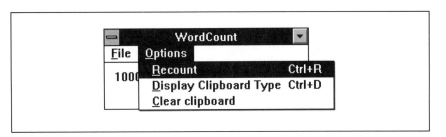

Notice that the WordCount application will recount if you press Ctrl-R, or display clipboard type if you press Ctrl-D.

Making the Keyboard Smarter with Telescoping

The keyboard doesn't *have* to be the antediluvian member of the input-tool pair. The next time you're building a list box, look at how the "Search" operates in Windows Help. There are perhaps hundreds of topics to search, but you're looking for the word *Mongolia*. You type **M** and the search list starts displaying only the items starting with *M*; you type **o**, and the list narrows to only the items starting with *Mo*, and so on. By the time you've typed **Mong**, you've probably narrowed the list to a few items, so you arrow down to *Mongolia*, press ↵, and you're done, and done more quickly than if you'd scrolled through hundreds of entries, with or without the mouse. This capability, called *telescoping* or *incremental searching*, also makes it much easier and faster to see if a given entry is even *in* the list; rather than having to scroll back and forth, you can see by typing a few letters whether the entry you are searching for exists.

Keyboard and Mouse Productivity Concerns

Before leaving keyboards, it's worth mentioning that complete keyboard implementation is important for reasons other than it's a nice thing to do. It's important because it makes your application a productivity tool.

GUIs make people more productive initially because you can get up and running quickly; that looks good. But compare the Word for Windows expert, who's clicking and dragging, to the WordPerfect 5.1 for DOS expert, who's taken the time to learn all those keystroke combinations.

The WordPerfect user is producing much more text. He had a much steeper learning curve, but once up there, he can crank out documents without trouble and with good speed.

How can the Word for Windows user compensate? Simple: There are shortcut keys for WinWord, as well. She just learns the WinWord shortcuts, and she's got the benefits of GUIs (terrific when doing something that she doesn't do all that often) as well as the productivity boost of being to do mainline work without the time lost to moving a hand from the keyboard to the mouse. But if there are no command-key alternatives, then she'll ultimately lose out to the DOS WordPerfect user in text output per hour.

Selection Techniques

Ensure that your application supports quick methods to select groups of text simply and easily.

Single Selection

As I said earlier, single selection is easy. But be sure that you know what kind of object can be selected. Is it a cell, a number, some text, an icon, an object in a drawing? If it's not obvious what kind of object can be selected, perhaps a prompt or a hint in the status area would be useful, assuming that you've implemented a status area. Or, better yet, try to implement the program to be as *modeless* as possible: Don't restrict what can be selected unless it's absolutely necessary to do so.

Group Selection

Group selection is usually accomplished by selecting the top of a group, then holding down the Shift key and moving the selection point (either the keyboard arrows or the mouse pointer) to the end of the group.

There should be visual feedback, usually the grouped items in highlight. For graphical items, that's represented with reversed colors.

OS/2 applications all support the Ctrl-/ and Ctrl-\ key combinations. Ctrl-/ selects all objects available (all items on a list, for example, or all icons in a window), Ctrl-\ *deselects* all items. The Windows File Manager supports those keys, although it's not documented that it does. Include those keys in *your* application.

Disjoint Selection

One place where GUIs really start to stand out from command-line applications is in their support of disjoint selection. Unfortunately, this is usually only supported from the mouse.

You can select just a few items from a list by holding down Ctrl and selectively clicking the items. You can see an example in Figure 4.3.

In Figure 4.3, you see a File Open box with a disjoint group of files selected. Again, there's no way to do that with the keyboard within the standard Windows style guides, but here's a

F I G U R E **4.3**

Selecting non-contiguous items from a list

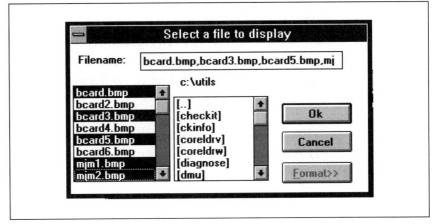

suggestion used in some non-Windows programs. Let the user use the cursor keys to move up and down in the list box, but then press the spacebar to select or deselect the item at the cursor.

Powerful Disjoint Selection

Until recently, applications supported disjoint selection only on list boxes. But a few applications are beginning to get more power on disjoint selection. Here's a few suggestions of disjoint data that it might make sense to be able to select.

- Multiple components of a drawing
- Cells of a spreadsheet
- Days in a scheduler
- Sections of text in a word processor

More and more, GUIs extend an object-oriented metaphor. It's terribly disappointing to get to the point where you just about start intuiting what an interface does, only to find that it doesn't quite make it when the metaphor is extended a bit.

Deselection

One last thought here: Be sure to provide for *deselection* abilities. If someone's gotten herself in some kind of corner, then perhaps the X key or a mouse click outside the selection area should deselect any selected items.

Summary Tables

Tables 4.1 to 4.6 show the recommendations made in the official Microsoft guide to Windows style; they summarize what keys and clicks to use for various functions.

T A B L E   **4.1:   Editing Keys**

KEY	RECOMMENDED FUNCTION
Del	If there is a selection, deletes entire selection.
	If there is an insertion point and no selection: Deletes character to *right* of insertion point.
Backspace	If there is a selection: Deletes entire selection.
	If there is an insertion point and no selection: Deletes character to *left* of insertion point.
Ins	Toggles between Insert mode (new text characters push old ones to right) and Overtype mode (new text characters overwrite old ones).

T A B L E   **4.2:**   **Modifier Keys**

KEY	TYPICAL FUNCTION
Shift	With alphanumeric keys, makes the character uppercase. (With Caps Lock on, yields lowercase characters.)
	With mouse click or navigation keys, defines the boundaries of the contiguous selection range.
	With function keys, alters meaning of action, allowing F1–F12 to become 12 more function keys.
Ctrl	With mouse-click, selects or deselects an item without affecting previous selections (disjoint selection and deselection).
	With alphabetic keys, provides shortcuts; for example, Ctrl-S often means "save file."
	With navigation keys, usually moves cursor by a larger unit than the unmodified key; for example, Home usually moves to the beginning of a line, but Ctrl-Home moves to the beginning of the document.
Alt	With alphabetic key, navigates to the menu or control marked with that key as a mnemonic.

T A B L E   **4.3:**   **Navigation Keys**

KEY	UNMODIFIED KEY MOVES CURSOR TO...	CTRL-KEY MOVES CURSOR TO...
Home	Beginning of line. (Leftmost position in current line.)	Beginning of data. (Top-left position in current field or document.)
End	End of line. (Rightmost position occupied by data in current line.)	End of data. (Bottom-right position occupied by data in current field or document.)
Page Up	Screen up. (Previous screen, same horizontal position.)	Screen left/beginning. (Top of window; or moves left one screen.)
Page Down	Screen down. (Next screen, same horizontal position.)	Screen right/end. (Bottom of window; or moves right one screen.)

T A B L E   **4.3:**   **Navigation Keys (continued)**

KEY	UNMODIFIED KEY MOVES CURSOR TO...	CTRL-KEY MOVES CURSOR TO...
←	Left one unit.	Left one (larger) unit.
→	Right one unit.	Right one (larger) unit.
↑	Up one unit/line.	Up one (larger) unit.
↓	Down one unit/line.	Down one (larger) unit.
Tab	Dialog boxes: Next field; may move left to right or top to bottom at designer's discretion; after last field, wraps to first. (Shift-Tab moves in the reverse order.)	(Not defined)

T A B L E   **4.4:**   **Standard PC Function Key Assignments**

KEY	(NO MODIFIER)	SHIFT	CTRL	ALT
F1	Help	Enter Help mode	N/A	N/A
F2	N/A	N/A	N/A	N/A
F3	Exit	N/A	N/A	N/A
F4	N/A	N/A	Close document window	Close application window
F5	N/A	N/A	N/A	N/A
F6	Move clockwise to next pane of active window	Move counter-clockwise to next pane of active window	Move to next document window; top window moves to bottom of stack. (Adding Shift reverses action: previous window moves to top.)	Move to application's next open non-document window. (Adding Shift reverses order of movement.)

T A B L E   **4.4:**   **Standard PC Function Key Assignments (continued)**

KEY	(NO MODIFIER)	SHIFT	CTRL	ALT
F7	N/A	N/A	N/A	N/A
F8	Toggle Extend mode, if supported.	Toggle Add mode, if supported.	N/A	N/A
F9	N/A	N/A	N/A	N/A
F10	Toggle menu bar activation.	(Supported for CUA 2.0 compatibility.)	N/A	N/A
F11, F12	N/A	N/A	N/A	N/A

T A B L E   **4.5:**   **Recommended Ctrl-Letter Shortcuts**

KEY	FUNCTION
Ctrl-Z, Alt-Backspace	Undo
Ctrl-X, Shift-Del	Cut
Ctrl-C, Ctrl-Ins	Copy
Ctrl-V, Shift-Ins	Paste

T A B L E **4.6:** **Suggested Ctrl-Letter Shortcuts**

KEY	FUNCTION
Ctrl-N	New
Ctrl-O	Open
Ctrl-P	Print
Ctrl-S	Save
Ctrl-B	Bold
Ctrl-I	Italic
Ctrl-U	Underline

USING

COLOR

C olor is an important part of any graphic environment. It's what people will notice first about your application,
even before they begin using its functions.

General GUI Color Design Principles

While this chapter isn't the cybernetic version of *Color Me
Beautiful*, there are a few basic rules that you can use to make
sure that you don't do the equivalent of putting plaid pants
and a striped shirt on your application.

Don't make the screen too bright or too dim. Use bright
colors for small areas, light colors for larger areas.

Provide visual cues. Use colors to group items. Objects have
a background color, a foreground color, and (often) a text
color. You can use these to draw the eye to something.

Don't count on a strong ability to distinguish color. Color
should not be a primary design cue, but instead a redundant
design cue; a large number of people have some kind of
color-sensory dysfunction. Not only do some users have the
familiar red-green colorblindness that some males are born
with, but also the lens of the eye yellows with age, making
distinguishing blue from white potentially more difficult for
any user over the age of 50. Put legends near data to enable
those with color dysfunctions to compare color value.

Make the colors customizable. Color has personal meaning,
so it should be customizable—unless, of course, the colors
are so essential that an important message would be missed
if the colors were goofed around with too much.

Don't get fancy. Stay with the basic 16 or 20 Windows colors. Each of those colors is either not dithered, or dithers well. (*Dithering* is how Windows displays a color that it cannot normally display. For example, the basic 16-color set of colors on a basic VGA driver does not contain a powder blue. A basic VGA driver will show powder blue as a combination of blues and whites. Close up, the blues and whites are obvious. From far way, however, they blend into a powder blue.) The basic Windows colors are as follows:

RED VALUE	GREEN VALUE	BLUE VALUE	RESULTING COLOR
0	0	0	Black
0	0	128	Cobalt Blue
0	255	0	Lime Green
0	255	255	Aqua ("Cyan")
128	0	0	Dark Red
128	128	0	Dark Yellow
255	0	0	Bright Red
255	0	255	Magenta
255	255	0	Bright Yellow
255	251	240	Light Yellow*
0	128	0	Dark green
0	0	255	Blue
192	220	192	Light Green*
0	128	128	Gray Blue/Green ("Dark Cyan")
128	0	128	Dark Purple

128	128	128	Dark Gray
164	200	240	Light Blue *
192	192	192	Gray
255	255	255	White
164	160	164	Medium Gray *

The colors with an asterisk indicate the four colors only available with 256-color drivers. These four colors will not dither in 256-color mode; they *will* in 16-color mode.

Color and Depth Perception

Windows makes much use of 3-D–like effects. As you know, 3-D is simulated by shading and perspective drawing. But did you know that color affects your perception of an object's depth? Figure 5.1 shows why.

FIGURE 5.1

How the eye sees color

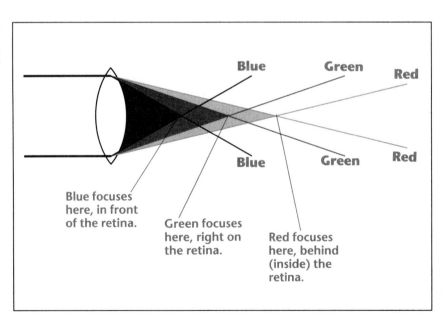

When white light, which is a combination of a number of different colors, goes through a lens, then the different colors—which are different *frequencies* of light—are bent; after all, that's how a lens works to focus light. But the different wavelengths bend at different rates, leading to a dispersion of colors. Now, it's not a *big* dispersion—*prisms* do big dispersion, but the lens in your eye isn't supposed to be a prism—but there *is* some dispersion. As a result, blue tones seem to be a bit farther away than do red tones. (This phenomenon is called *chromostereopsis*.)

Use that phenomenon when coloring objects on a computer screen. Blue will seem far away, and red will seem near. Therefore, if you're using two colored objects that overlie one another, the one on the bottom will look more natural if it is blue. More specifically, the following should be the order from nearest to farthest when using different numbers of colors.

NUMBER OF COLORS	ORDER IN WHICH THE COLOR SHOULD APPEAR, NEAREST TO FARTHEST
2	red, blue *or* yellow, blue
3	either red, green, and blue; *or* red, yellow, and blue
4	red, yellow, green, blue
5	red, orange, yellow, green, blue
6	red, orange, yellow, green, blue, purple

It also means that you should not present blue and red text together against a dark background; the differences in apparent depth will look jarring.

Color Guidelines

It's tempting to go overboard when selecting colors for an application, but too much variety will distract your user and make your application less easy to use. These are general rules for using colors:

Keep it simple. Use as few colors as possible. It's simpler to grasp, and simpler to distinguish on lesser-quality output devices.

Use contrasting colors as measuring tools. If you plan to use color to indicate a continuum, like the passage of time when waiting for some task to finish, or perhaps a range of some physical constant, then do *not* use a spectrum to do it. After all, most of us wouldn't perceive violet as the opposite of red, but it is the color opposite red on the spectrum of Red, Orange, Yellow, Green, Blue, Indigo, Violet. Turning a square from red to orange to yellow to green to blue to indigo to violet to indicate time required to, say, format a floppy would tell your user nothing. Instead, use two different primary colors, like red and blue, and use color gradations between them to indicate progress.

Don't give users too much to remember. If colors should have a meaning (e.g., red are style sheets, blue are documents, green are graphics files), then don't use more than five colors. Even though a picture is worth a thousand words, people can remember the items on a seven-option word menu better than they can five colors in an array of file types.

Do use color, however, to help people recognize things. It wouldn't be a bad idea if the File Manager allowed you to assign colors to particular file extensions. You wouldn't need to color *every* file icon, but it might be nice to be able to set off spreadsheets and documents the way that subdirectories are set off.

Again, this issue is a case of "if you're going to do it, do it right." Badly used colors can be worse than no colors. In one study, researchers asked people to pick out triangles from rectangles on a computer screen. The researchers first tested subjects who viewed a monochrome screen, then they tested subjects using a color screen wherein the triangles were colored with one color, and the rectangles were colored in another color. The study found that when color was added to a display of objects, then particular objects became easier to find, as you'd imagine. But then they tested people on color screens where the color had nothing to do with the recognition task—and the search/discrimination time *rose*. Moral of the story: Good color makes screens better, but bad color is worse than no color at all.

In a similar study, one test group was asked to separate triangles from rectangles, and they were advised beforehand that the triangles would be red and the rectangles blue. They were the fastest group of all.

Organize with color. Use color to group things, as in the previous example.

Keep common associations. When associating colors with events, use commonly recognized color associations. For example:

- ▶ red usually means danger, error, or higher temperature
- ▶ yellow usually means caution or warning
- ▶ blue may mean cooler temperature

This underscores a previous point about color opposites. When red means "stop," then its opposite is green, which means "go." In contrast, when red means "high temperature," then its opposite is blue, which means " lower temperature."

In addition, when using a lot of colors, provide a legend to help people remember which colors associate with what ideas. Perhaps use a floating dialog box that can be hidden once the user has memorized the colors.

- When coloring words or menu options, do not use one color to indicate a hotkey or shortcut key. The perceived differences in depth (chromostereopsis, recall?) that result can slow reading speed considerably. If you want to use a different color for a command, use the color for the entire command name.

Cultural Meanings of Colors

If your product is to have international appeal, you should be aware that Western perceptions of color are not echoed all throughout the world. For example, in Japan, the bad guys wear *blue* hats; in Egypt, yellow is the color of happiness and prosperity. It's hard to make combinations that will please everybody, but this is one more argument for making your colors customizable.

Choosing Background/Foreground Colors

In general, choose background and foreground colors from complementary pairs of colors to assure readability.

Colors are described not only by their hue (red, blue, green, etc.) but also by their purity. Take a deep red and add some blue and green, and it becomes pastel. A pure color is said to be *saturated*. A less pure color is said to be (logically enough) *desaturated*.

- When choosing a foreground and a background, don't choose color pairs that are both light, or both dark. They don't contrast enough.

- Choose pairs that are chromatically complementary; in other words, colors which when added together will yield white, like yellow and blue.

- In general, when choosing foreground and background colors, you'll have good luck if you choose pairs that are different in hue, shade, and intensity.

- When working with a white background, use saturated or pure colors for your lettering.

- When working with a black background, use desaturated (pastel) colors.

Don't take your cues from modern advertising and periodical art; there's a lot of experimentation going on right now. You're not trying to be avante garde; you're trying to be readable. Save the light-cerise-and-pale-aqua combinations for future, larger, higher quality monitors—if they ever appear on the market. Remember, you seek to build a GUI program that *won't* be noticed.

Colors and Size

The colors that you choose can cause illusions for your readers about size; keep these things in mind when designing with color:

- Colors in small areas are difficult to distinguish. Put small black letters next to small blue letters, and it may be impossible to tell that they are different colors.

- Equal-sized areas look larger when they are in brighter colors. A brighter icon, control, or bitmap will look a different size than a darker one, even if they are next to one another.

- Use the highest-contrast colors (dark on white background, light on black background) for detailed diagrams. Remember that the most legible color combination is often black on white.

Lighting and 3-D

You may never have noticed it, but objects in the Windows world are lit from the near upper left, from over the user's left shoulder, along a diagonal to far lower right, behind the monitor. In particular, remember these rules:

- Shadows should fall to the right and behind the object from the user's point of view.

- 3-D objects should face to the left obliquely.

- Flat objects should have a shadow.

Look at some of the icons in Figure 5.2 and you'll see how this should work.

FIGURE **5.2**

Well-drawn vs. poorly-drawn icons

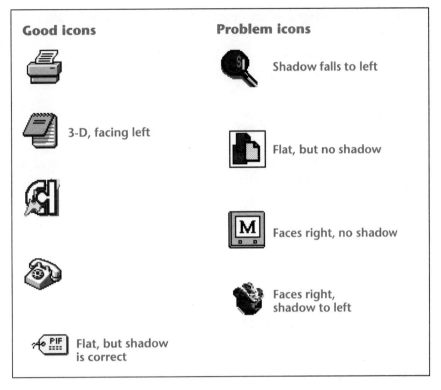

FIGURE **5.2**

Well-drawn vs. poorly-drawn icons

And when designing icons, think about *not* designing icons. Getting those little 32-by-32 critters right is the job for an experienced graphic designer. Silly as it sounds, people are either impressed or turned off by your icons. Company logos are good when rendered right, as they end up being small thumbnail sketches of larger pictures that your users have seen previously. And forget the simple geometric figures—they've been used before, and they're played out. Unfortunately, modern icons have to be 3-D, properly colored, properly anti-aliased (see the next section), and properly shaded, or you look bush league. For an example, look at the top icon on the right-hand side of Figure 5.2, and look at the third icon down from the top on the left-hand side. They are the icons used in the original and current versions of a nifty little utility called SCSI Scan. The original magnifying glass icon was pretty lame, but the new icon, based on the Adaptec (the makers of the utility) logo, looks pretty professional.

Sharpening and Blurring Edges

Dialog boxes should have a nice sharp edge to them. Icons often should *not* have an edge. Figures 5.3 and 5.4 demonstrate first a dialog box before and after anti-aliasing, and then a magnification of a bitmap before and after anti-aliasing.

F I G U R E **5.3**

A situation in which anti-aliasing is a bad idea—the sharp dialog box (top) looks disheveled and blurred after anti-aliasing (bottom).

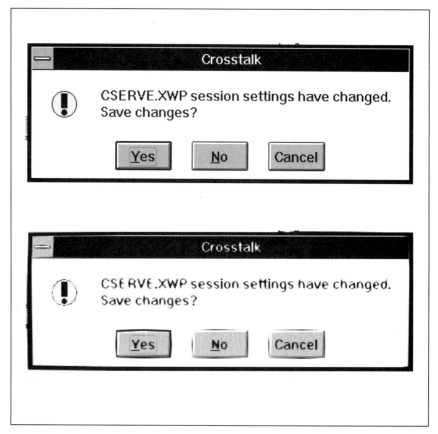

You can see that in the case of the dialog box, anti-aliasing was a bad idea. But look at the two greatly-enlarged bitmaps in Figure 5.4 to see the result after anti-aliasing.

The original bitmap of a planetary outline looked jaggy; the perpendicular look to the coastlines weren't believable. After anti-aliasing, however, they had a nice, smooth look that seemed kind of natural. If I showed you both original bitmaps on the printed page, you wouldn't see much difference; that's why I'm showing you the magnified versions to see what anti-aliasing does. Basically, it gets rid of "the jaggies," a phenomenon that occurs when putting angled lines on a bitmapped medium.

How does anti-aliasing work? It's an optical illusion. Sharply defined curves look "jaggy" on a pixel screen. A black curve against a white background will look awful. Anti-aliasing smooths out the look of the curve by *gradually* changing the colors; instead of black on white, it rebuilds the image to show white, then light gray, then dark gray, and finally black.

Further Reading

Color is a big subject; to learn more, take a look at *Using Computer Color Effectively: An Illustrated Resource*, by Lisa G. Thorell and Wanda J. Smith, published by Prentice-Hall in 1990. I apologize to those authors if I have been too free in my borrowings and adaptations. I highly recommend this book; when researching this material, I read four books specifically written about computer color. I found *Using Computer Color Effectively* to be the best of them by far, and indeed I found the other three to be of no value whatsoever.

F I G U R E   **5.4**

A situation in which anti-aliasing is a good idea— the jaggy bitmap (top) looks much smoother after anti-aliasing (bottom).

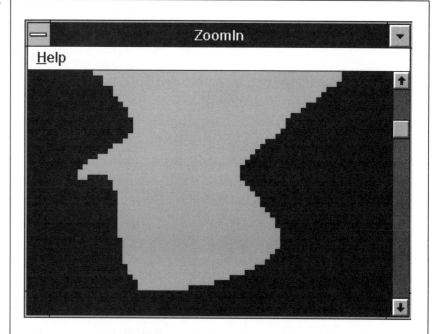

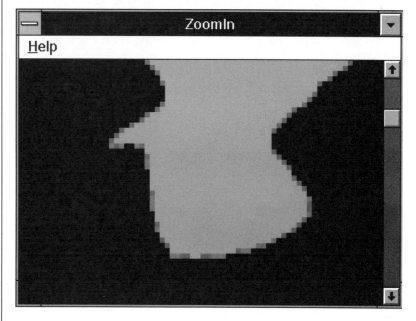

CONSTRUCTING

USEFUL

MENUS

A good menu structure makes your program easy to learn, easy to use infrequently (that is, you don't need to be in practice to use it effectively), and fun to explore. A bad menu structure invites words like *maze*, *labyrinth*, and *jungle*.

Menu Types

Within the programming models of Windows and most other GUIs, you'll find four kinds of menus:

- Drop-down
- Cascaded
- Pop-up or floating
- Tear-off

Each kind of menu has special uses.

Drop-Down Menus

The drop-down menu is the basic type of menu in most GUIs. Stemming from a title in the menu bar, it looks like Figure 6.1.

This is the oldest menu type in the GUI world, and it can serve admirably as the only menu in your application, if the application will only use one menu type. To keep your menus from getting too complicated-looking, you can divide them into sections with horizontal crossbars or use cascaded or pop-up menus. If you choose to divide your menus with crossbars

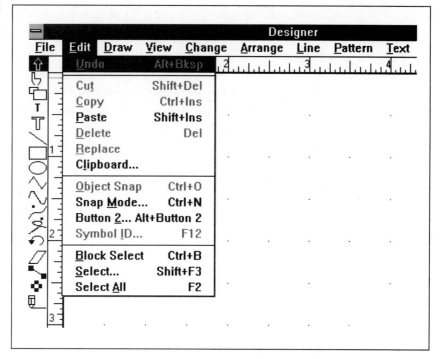

(and, if you've got more than about three or four entries, you really should), be sure to group menu items according to function. Place no more than three or four entries in each section.

Graying Out Options

Menus can contain options that only work under certain circumstances. When a menu option is not valid, it can (under the control of your program) be *grayed out*. When grayed out, an option appears on the menu, but clicking on it won't do anything.

The whole idea of graying out is a pretty good one, as it indicates what's possible in an application and encourages exploration of the application. But graying out can be frustrating, as sometimes a grayed-out option can be *just the thing* that you're looking for. Perhaps clicking a grayed-out item should bring up a dialog box explaining under what circumstances the item would be enabled. ("Enabled" is the opposite of "grayed out;" I suppose the opposite of "grayed out" should be "blacked in," but I've never heard the term used.)

Indicating More Depth in Choices

Sometimes menu items will require more information or have more options attached than are readily visible from the drop-down menu. If menu items lead to either cascaded menus (see below) or dialog boxes, you should indicate this in the menu. Generally, a cascaded menu is indicated by a right-facing triangle, and a dialog box by an ellipsis ("..."). It's important to do this, so that the user knows that if he clicks on an option that does *not* have a triangle or ellipsis after it, he will be selecting that option.

Drop-down windows—the dialog box that results from clicking a menu item ending in an ellipsis—should have title-bar text that matches the text on the original menu item. As always, these titles should be as descriptive of what's on the menu as possible.

Cascaded Menus

Cascaded menus branch from an option in a standard menu. They appear off to the right side of the drop-down menu option, as you see in Figure 6.2.

FIGURE **6.2**

A cascaded menu

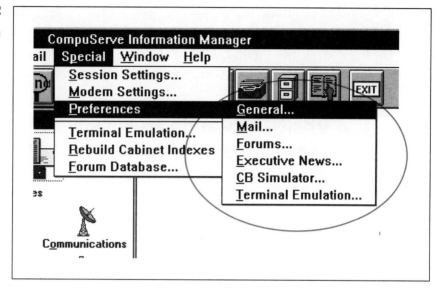

FIGURE **6.2**

A cascaded menu

Windows uses a right-pointing triangle to indicate that a standard menu option leads to a cascading menu. Don't overuse cascading menus. They're an extra step to get to (possibly preventing some users from ever discovering some capabilities of your application), and I've seen some applications that put cascading menus on top of cascading menus to produce a *real* challenge of a menu system.

Advantages of Cascading Menus

Cascading menus can offer the following positive features:

- The drop-down menu structure can be simplified, as you saw in the preceding figure. All of the setup options could be accessed with a single line on the drop-down menu, which in turn lead to the cascaded menu.

- If you alert the user (in the Help) to the fact that they can browse the cascading menus by dragging the mouse over the menu system, then you will offer your user access to a lot of features in an easy-to-browse format.

Disadvantages of Cascading Menus

In general, cascading menus offer more down-sides than they do benefits, so consider these things when deciding whether or not to use them.

- Cascaded menus are a bit trickier to get to from the mouse or the keyboard than are normal standard menus.

- They make it harder for the user to browse commands, as she can't see all the menu items simply by dragging the mouse across the menu bar.

- They add complexity to a menu structure. If your menu structure seems *that* complex, consider redesigning it to make better use of options and dialog boxes.

Cascading menus titles are displayed in the same way as the parent window item.

Pop-Up Menus

Recent Microsoft applications have used *pop-up* menus activated by the right mouse button, as you see in Figure 6.3.

The pop-up menu is very useful for getting to commonly-used functions like, in the case of Excel, copy and paste and cell-formatting commands. Pop-up menus also have the advantage of conserving space, as the menu doesn't appear until you ask

FIGURE **6.3**

A pop-up menu

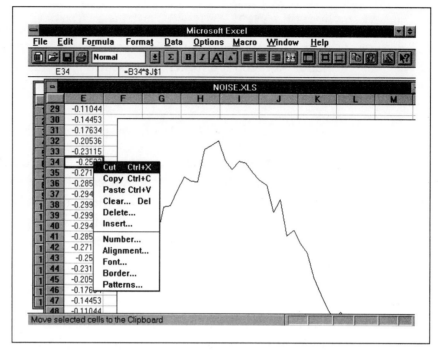

for it. Not everyone likes using the right mouse button, however, so don't make it mandatory for any command. Pop-up menus are a bit off-putting to some people because *they don't stay put*. Once they're up, then you'd better make some kind of decision, and do it *now*, because with your next mouse click, the menu will disappear.

Put It Near the Mouse, but Not Too Near

If using a pop-up menu, make sure that it doesn't sit *too* near the mouse's hotspot. If it appears too close, then it'll be too easy for your user to accidentally activate an option on the menu. That doesn't imply that the menu should be off on the other side of the screen, however; the whole idea of the pop-up menu is convenience.

Limit What You Put on the Pop-Up

The pop-up menu is supposed to be an easy-to-use convenience, so keep it simple. No cascading menus here, and limit the number of items on the pop-up to about seven.

Make the Pop-Up User-Definable

One of the best things that you could do with a pop-up menu would be to offer two or three user-definable slots on the menu. You'd just show the user the items that appear on your application's menu, and then give her the option to drag any of those items into the pop-up menu.

Tear-Off Menus

Tear-off menus are not used in Windows; they appear in some OS/2 applications. A tear-off menu is a cascade or pop-up menu that you can click on and drag to somewhere else on the screen, "tearing off" its original location.

Tear-off menus can be used as a kind of halfway point between a submenu structure and a dialog box.

Standard Windows Menus

Windows users have come to expect certain menus. Start from these examples, and people will feel immediately comfortable with your program. Again, you're trying to build a program that people *won't* notice. Figure 6.4 shows a standard menu.

This is by *no means* a recommendation to use this menu, and only this menu. It's just a starting point. The File, Edit, and Options menus should appear pretty much all of the time.

FIGURE 6.4

A standard window with no menus activated

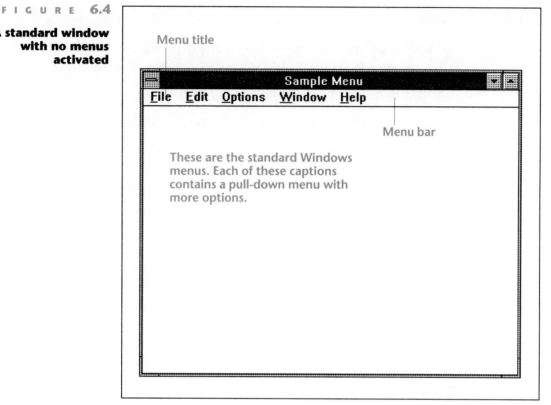

Menu title

Menu bar

These are the standard Windows menus. Each of these captions contains a pull-down menu with more options.

(Remember that you can break any rule that you like, so long as, first, you're aware that you're breaking the rule and, second, you're aware *why* you're breaking the rule.) The Window menu only appears if you're using the MDI (Multiple Document Interface) to support multiple windows inside the main program. Help is, one hopes, *de rigeur*, but some programs place it flush right against the right side of the menu bar. That was the rule in Windows programs until Windows 3.1; at that point, Microsoft started recommending that it be flush left with the other menu items, but that it be the rightmost menu item.

The File Menu

The File Menu (see Figure 6.5) is the one that speaks to the outside world: It reads and writes files, controls printers, and exits the program, at a minimum.

You need a file menu if your application supports stored objects. Most of the items are self-explanatory. Actually, several

You need a File menu if the application supports stored objects.

Sample Menu

File Edit Options Window Help

New —————————— Accelerator key: Ctrl-N
Open... ————————— Accelerator key: Ctrl-O
Close
Save ————————— Accelerator key: Ctrl-S
Save As...
Print... ————————— Accelerator key: Ctrl-P
Page Setup...
Print Setup... ————— The ellipsis indicates that there is a dialog box with more options attached to the window.

1 DATAF.DOC
2 MYFILE.TXT
3 JUNKFILE.DOC ———— Names of recently used files
4 GOODFILE.DOC

Exit

Notice the underlined letters in the menus and their options. If you press Alt+that letter, you can select that option with the keyboard.

of the items in the File menu are mainly done for you *automatically* by the Windows environment via the "common dialog boxes," pre-built dialog boxes that you can call with very little work (they're covered later, in Chapter 8). There's a File Open dialog, a "Save" dialog, a "Choose Printer" dialog, and a "Page Setup" dialog.

Additionally, it's become fashionable to include the last three to five retrieved objects' names on the File menu so that recently-used files can be easily reopened. (This section is called the *MRU* section, for Most Recently Used.) It's a great idea, and users love it; include it in your system, and make it flexible— if your users want to remember their last nine documents, let them!

The Edit Menu

If at all possible, your application should support the Clipboard, and DDE and OLE support is becoming less and less "optional" among Windows applications. The Edit menu (see Figure 6.6) is where all those functions are accessed.

This particular Edit menu is a bit full; you probably wouldn't have all those items on a single menu in reality. Instead, this is an amalgam of different Edit menus.

Notice that the keystrokes for Cut, Copy, and Paste are Ctrl-X, Ctrl-C, and Ctrl-V. Until recently, the accelerators were Shift-Del= for Cut, Ctrl-Ins for Copy, and Shif-Ins for Paste. The new keys aren't mnemonic, so where did they come from? Look at the keyboard, and you'll see where they came from. X, C, and V are right next to each other, and they're easy-to-get-to keys. The Macintosh uses them for Cut, Copy, and Paste as well; that's where the idea came from in the first place.

FIGURE 6.6

A standard window with the Edit menu activated

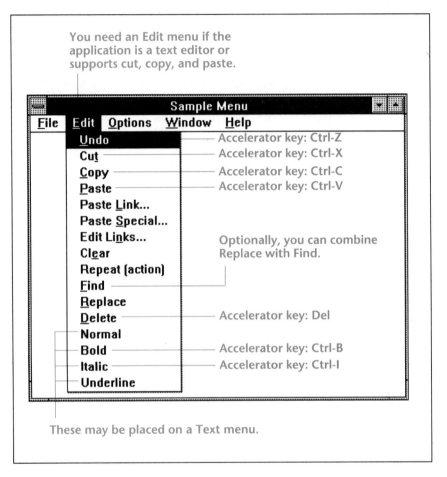

You need an Edit menu if the application is a text editor or supports cut, copy, and paste.

These may be placed on a Text menu.

The Options Menu

It's hard to offer generic information for this menu, as it will almost by definition be different for each program. Many applications will not even have an options menu labeled as such, but will divide such functions under menus such as Tools or Style. Figure 6.7 shows an Options menu.

FIGURE 6.7

**A standard window
with the Options
menu activated**

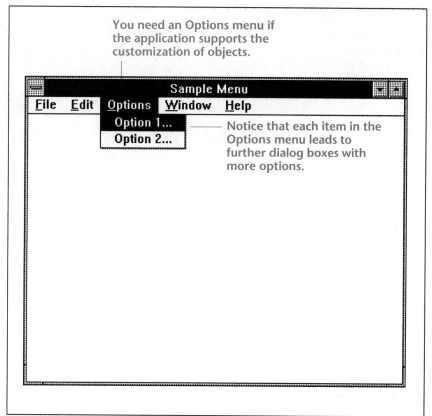

The Windows Menu

Many Windows programs support MDI. To work, it needs a menu like the one shown in Figure 6.8.

Within MDI, there is one window that is the "focus" or "foreground" window. That will be indicated on the menu with a check mark. The Tile and Cascade functions (which allow the user to select how the windows are displayed) are very important; don't leave them out.

**A standard menu
with the Window
menu activated**

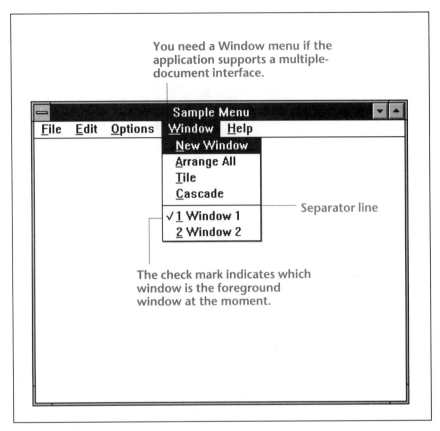

You need a Window menu if the
application supports a multiple-
document interface.

Separator line

The check mark indicates which
window is the foreground
window at the moment.

Menu Items

The sorts of things that your users will see on a menu vary.
There are several different kinds of menu items:

- actions (such as Open)
- attributes (such as Italic)
- documents

- document windows (as used in a MDI-capable application)

- graphical menu items (such as the tools in a toolbox)

Some menu items take effect as soon as they are selected, but others require further information. Any command that requires more information to run is called a *dialog box command,* as clicking on its menu item produces a dialog box. It's probably a good idea to make dangerous (i.e., destructive) commands such as Delete or Format dialog box commands, just to make sure that the user didn't click on that menu item accidentally; it gives you a chance to confirm the action with the user before blowing away his data. (At the same time, you should offer the option to skip the confirmations and just do the action.) If a menu item will sometimes have a dialog box attached and sometimes take effect immediately (depending on the situation), it's better to leave off the ellipsis altogether, so that the user will never expect a dialog box (complete with Cancel button) when there isn't one.

Independent vs. Interdependent

Some menu items are *independent,* while others are *interdependent.* Independent menu items are the equivalent of checkboxes in a dialog box, where you can select more than one option at any time. For example, text attributes (such as Italic) are independent, as you can change one text attribute without changing all the others.

Interdependent menu items work more like radio buttons, of which you can only select one at a time. If your application can display the document at a number of different sizes (such as Full Page, Standard, and Custom) for easier editing, each of those display options is an interdependent menu item, as you can't pick more than one at a time. You can see a further discussion on controls—including check boxes and radio buttons—in Chapter 7.

Menu Guidelines

The key to good menus is organization. If your users can be pretty sure ahead of time where a given choice will be, the hotkey to select it and what other choices it will be near, they'll find your application easier to use.

Creating Good Menu Titles

Always define an mnemonic (e.g., Alt-something or Ctrl-something) for menu items. To be effective, this mnemonic should be one that the user is likely to associate with that word. In order of selection preference:

- If possible, use the first character of the menu item as the mnemonic.

- If you can't use the first letter of a command, and the command has two words, use the first letter of the second word.

- If that's not possible, try the next consonant in the menu title.

- If you still can't get a mnemonic that doesn't conflict, use the first available vowel.

After selecting the mnemonic, indicate what that key is next to the menu entry. All the access keys in a particular menu should be different, but you can use the same key combination in different menus.

As I've said, some menu items will point to cascading menus or dialog boxes, and you should use an ellipsis (...) to indicate that the action will not take place immediately.

Designing a Good Menu

Here are a few suggestions on how to *place* and *group* items on a menu to maximize its effectiveness:

> **Group items:** Use the separators to create logical groupings within menus. Don't let menus just run on with a dozen submenu items without offering the eye and the brain some grouping clues.
>
> **Be careful about placement:** Look carefully at the options that you're placing next to each other. Take a look at the Windows game's menu in Figure 6.9 for an example.

In the game that the menu in Figure 6.9 is taken from, it's fairly common to build ships. But one misclick (one you may not even notice), and you're mothballing your fleets. With Romulans waiting behind every asteroid, this is hardly a good thing…. Seriously, though, I've seen commercial applications that blithely place dangerous options right next to commonly-used ones; don't do that.

By the way, before you get a bad impression of this game— Spaceward Ho!—*don't*. The menu structure isn't very good,

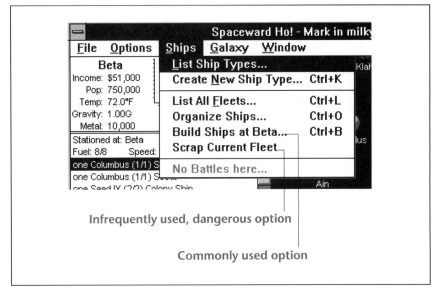

Infrequently used, dangerous option

Commonly used option

but then you don't need it for most of what you do in Spaceward Ho!. For example, I never build ships—the example that I just cited—by clicking on the menu. I can, instead, just double-click on the planet that I wish to build ships on, and the Build Ships dialog box appears automatically. To start a ship on a journey from one planet to another, you just click and drag the ship from source to destination; a line with an arrow at the end indicates the starting and ending point. If the ship can't make the journey because it doesn't have enough fuel, then the line's color changes, as a cue that you "can't get there from here." Those are a couple of excellent examples of using the mouse in a somewhat object-like manner. (If looking at a game seems silly, it isn't—games often form the vanguard in user interfaces.)

Provide shortcuts. As I've said before, anything important on a menu should have a shortcut or accelerator key. (Alt-, Ctrl-Alt, etc.).

However, avoid Alt with a number key: Although it's possible to do this under Windows, do not use an Alt-key combination for an accelerator key; it should be a mnemonic.

Provide "beginner" and "advanced" menus. Offer long menus and short menus so that people can either use the application in a limited but simple mode (short menus) or a more complex but more powerful mode (long menus).

Don't make them guess if the feature actually works. If a menu item is not available, gray it out. Make sure that it's clear that it's not an accident that that option isn't available, however. It is possible to change the menu text on the fly, which means that you could simply remove some text from the menu altogether when its option isn't working, but don't; instead, gray them out.

Provide status indicators: Use check marks to indicate when a mode (like Bold or Auto Arrange) is selected, or which window has the focus in an MDI application's Window menu.

Don't change the menu: Do not modify the menu when the Shift, Ctrl, or Alt keys are depressed—when the user presses the Shift key, for example, the menus that appear in the application window should not change.

USING

TEXT

IN

A

GUI

APPLICATION

*E*ven though a picture's worth a thousand words, words are still important in a graphical environment. In this chapter, we'll examine how to make the best use of the small space that you have for getting your message across.

Screen Text Is Different from Paper Text

Before Windows and Macs, most computer screens showed white letters on a black background. Windows and other GUIs, however, seem to show black text on a white background. Why is this? Because they're trying to look like *paper*.

It's a noble goal, but there are two things wrong with it:

- paper isn't luminous
- ink on paper is usually pretty high-resolution

I've heard Windows text referred to as the "lightbulb video model," because reading Windows text is like trying to read the wattage on a lightbulb that's turned on. Newer high-resolution screens have made that less of a problem, but even the highest-resolution screen is still only about dot matrix–level in quality.

Given that your medium (the screen) is a quite imperfect one, you've got an interest in keeping your text simple and non-distracting. To that end:

Strive for clarity. Avoid technical explanations. Explain whatever needs the user's attention in as clear a manner as is possible. Don't spend so much time explaining the problem—that's often whining and rationalization. Explain how to *solve* the problem.

Take time to handle plurals. Take a few more lines of code to handle plurals correctly. I find it annoying that DOS has grown from 10K to 70K in size, and still Microsoft apparently thinks that it would be too much trouble to differentiate between the word "file" and "files". To see what I mean, copy a file in DOS. The result is "one file(s) copied". It's unprofessional.

Avoid the first person. Programs should refer to themselves in the third person. "Designer is unable to …" is better than "I am unable to…" as text in a message. The use of the first person was a style at one time in the computer business, but it's not used as much. Why? Simple: In user interfaces, it was thought that by making a dialog with the computer seem somewhat like a dialog with a human, the computer would be easier to "relate to," making the interface "user friendly." We might call this the "conversational model" of user dialog.

The whole idea backfires, however, because the computer's range of possible responses is very narrow. *If this thing is a conversationalist*, you think, *then it's not much of one!* Devices don't have to be chatty in order to be effective. Take, for example, your VCR. It does some mildly complex things, but there's nothing in its user interface that leads you to think that it can tell you about the weather, or even whether or not a particular TV show will be worth taping, or why your reception is lousy. The VCR sets your expectations early by saying, "this is what I do, and it's *all* I do; don't expect any nifty hidden features." In contrast, imagine if you programmed a VCR by talking to it:

"VCR?" you start off.

"Working…" comes the reply.

"Tape *Next Generation* for me, okay?"

"I do not understand," it answers. "Your messages must be formulated like so: Say the word 'tape,' followed by the channel number, followed by the starting time and date in English format, followed by the program duration."

This would be awfully frustrating. Unless you say "tape channel 20 from seven P.M. on Saturday for one hour," it has no idea what you're asking it to do. The voice input is useless. In contrast, if the program did not work in the first person, and just prompted you for time, date, and channel, then it would be harder to misunderstand it, the user would "get it right" more often, and the VCR would more useful.

In sum, a computer program using "I" to refer to itself seems to promise some intelligence under the hood. Don't make promises that you can't keep.

> **Keep it brief.** Keep the message short. If you can't keep the message short, then keep the box no more than about three inches wide (for readability's sake) and provide more-than-normal spacing between the lines.
>
> **Be explicit about problems and solutions.** Refer specifically to what the user can do to repair the problem— "XYZ cannot write to A: drive because the floppy in A: is write protected. Remove the floppy, move the write

protect tab to the *unprotect* position, reinsert the floppy, and press Retry." Along the same lines, don't say "Insufficient room on A: to store file"; instead, say "Insufficient room on A: to store file; X bytes required, Y bytes available." Name the file, as this helps with troubleshooting.

Watch terminology. When writing dialog boxes, there are some standard words you should use in the interests of consistency, and there are some other words you should avoid. For example:

▶ When telling people to press a key, use the word "press;" it's not perfect, but it seems the best of the lot. Some people object to "strike a key," and being told to "depress" a key sounds like you should tell it that it's ugly and its mother dresses it funny. "Touch" a key sounds a bit tentative— to me, touching and pressing are quite different things.

▶ When asking if a program or process should cut itself short, avoid "terminate" and "abort;" instead, try "end process now?" or "stop formatting now?" or something like that.

▶ Be sure to differentiate between when something can be cancelled, and when something can only be stopped. Whenever possible, offer an "undo" function.

▶ Do not use message/error numbers. They look too much like debug output that never got taken out of the code.

▶ Avoid the word "error." You're not trying to make someone feel stupid or inadequate for using your product

Be careful about grammar and vocabulary. Dialog boxes keep appearing in front of the user, so any grammatical errors or strange words will also keep appearing in front of her.

▶ Have someone proofread your dialog boxes for wrong words and, again, misspellings. In particular, be careful for misuse of the use of apostrophes in possessive phrases. When I talk about this in class, techies invariably get up in arms; they often seem to think that proper grammar and spelling is just pointless lagniappe, the needless consistency that is claimed to be the hobgoblin of small minds.

Reader, if you're one of those people, I've just got to tell you: It just isn't true. People see a grammatical or spelling error, and their estimate of your IQ drops about 30 points. They mutter, "Didn't these idiots even bother to spell-check the thing?"

Spelling counts, and grammar counts. You're trying to make the readable areas of your program read as smoothly as possible; errors are like speed bumps on the road to most readers.

▶ Furthermore, hire a technical editor to go over your dialog boxes and messages. Previously, I recommended getting the services of a graphics designer to build your icons; get a professional to help you with *text*, too. There is no dishonor in this—after all, if you're a program designer, then being a program designer is your area of expertise; no one expects you to be a graphics expert and a professional writer too. Do you feel stupid or inadequate if you hire someone else to do expert carpentry on your house, or auto repair on your car? *I* don't—I'm not someone who cuts boards or turns a wrench for a living, and it seems to me that if I want something done right, I'd do well to go to someone who *does* do those things for many hours each week. If I redid my den, I'd certainly save money; but, then, my den would also *look* like I redid it. You should think in the same way for icons and messages.

- Avoid jargon. There are fewer and fewer computer experts out in the user community. More and more computer users think RAM has horns. Folks shouldn't need a computer glossary to run your program.

- Avoid slang; when presented by a computer, expressions containing slang are jarring.

- Along the same lines, avoid terminology that could be seen as being culturally specific. Most people know what an "expert" is, so offering "expert" menus probably wouldn't confuse anyone. But offering "maven" or "boffin" menus would be taken as a bit odd.

- While contractions are fine—often preferred, in fact—in much written speech, they shouldn't be used in messages. Compare:

"If you press OK, XYZAPP cannot undo this operation."

with

"If you press OK, XYZAPP can't undo this operation."

Phrase questions unambiguously. On your button tops, be careful not to ask any "How long have you been beating your wife?" questions. Imagine dialog boxes with these texts in them, and buttons that just say OK or Cancel:

▸ "This will overwrite existing file. Cancel?"

▸ "Saving to another file will preserve existing file. Save to another file instead?"

What is the second one asking? If I press OK, does that save to a file with a different name? What does Cancel do—cancel the whole operation, or cancel the "save as" and just execute the "save"? By the way, both of those messages come from actual Windows applications.

Presenting Text In Messages

While long messages are to be avoided, they can't be stomped out altogether. Consider the message shown in Figure 7.1.

Try reading that in comparison to Figure 7.2:

Although neither one is terribly desirable, the second one is more accessible. And please don't do what I've done in Figure 7.3.

The general rule is: Avoid the gimmicks, and make your text look like a newspaper or magazine column. That'll help readability as much as possible.

F I G U R E 7.1

A dialog box with poorly arranged text

> **Box with lines too long**
>
> This is an example of a dialog box that uses lines that run on for too long. It can be quite difficult for a reader to follow lines that run too wide without any kind of a break. The ways to combat the natural difficulty of reading this dialog box include increasing the interline spacing, or LEADING, of the text. Another way to improve readability is to make the columns more narrow. Remember that screens are harder to read than are sheets of paper, and make it easier for your users to figure out what you mean – and they'll like your application better.

> **Easier-to-read box**
>
> This is an example of a dialog box that
> is a bit easier to read. It can be quite
> difficult for a reader to follow lines that
> run too wide without any kind of a break.
> The ways to combat the natural difficulty
> of reading this dialog box include
> increasing the interline spacing, or
> LEADING, of the text. Another way to
> improve readability is to make the
> columns more narrow. Remember that
> screens are harder to read than are
> sheets of paper, and make it easier for
> your users to figure out what you mean –
> and they'll like your application better.
> Unfortunately, in Windows there is no
> simple way to increase leading.

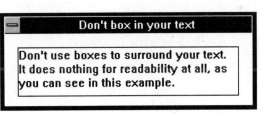

> **Don't box in your text**
>
> Don't use boxes to surround your text.
> It does nothing for readability at all, as
> you can see in this example.

Editing Text

Your program will have to support the ability to edit text in
text fields. It may seem like a small thing, but one of the most
potentially annoying things that a program can do is to behave counterintuitively when deleting text. Here are the rules

for editing text in most GUI environments:

- The Backspace key should delete the character to the *left*.

- As the Backspace key deletes, it should drag the text to the right of it over to the left one character.

- Backspacing at the extreme left edge of the edit area should join the current line and the one above it, if there is one.

- The Del or Delete key should delete the character to the *right*, and, as with the Backspace key, should drag the text to its right over to the left.

- If the Del key is in the extreme right-hand position on a line when it is pressed, then the current line and the one below it should be joined.

- Text editing should be reversible with the Alt-Q (undo) keystroke, and the Ctrl-U key combination, unless the text application needs to use Ctrl-U for underlining.

Fonts in a GUI Environment

The Windows, Macintosh, and OS/2 environments support hundreds of different typefaces. As a result, you can build applications using dozens of fonts.

Unfortunately.

People expect to see Windows messages in 10-point System font or 8-point MS Sans Serif. Anything else looks strange, as you see in Figure 7.4.

FIGURE 7.4

Why you should stick with the System font

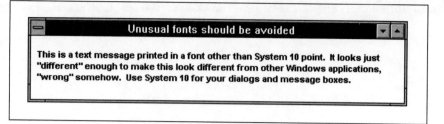

The temptation to exploit fonts is difficult to resist, but *resist.* Take, for example, this block of text in a font called Tekton. It is based on the handwriting of an architect living in Seattle. ("Tekton" is Greek for "to build"—get it?) For informal writing, it's really neat—so neat, in fact, that many people in my office actually write memos in it. Read a few paragraphs of this, however, and you'll get the point driven home that it's just plain not as easy to read as is a normal text face like Arial (Helvetica), Times Roman, Palatino, Optima, or the like.

A Point Isn't Necessarily a Point

When comparing text font sizes, most people think that all 12-point fonts are the same height. It's not true at all. Compare, for example, the fonts in Figure 7.5.

Since most Windows fonts are proportional, mixing fonts can lead to tables not lining up correctly—another reason to stay with a single font family for dialogs and menus.

FIGURE 7.5

Different fonts have significantly different heights at the same point size.

A line of 12-point Joanna

A line of 12-point Times Roman

A line of 12-point Arial

A line of 12-point Avant Garde

CHAPTER 8

DESIGNING

DIALOG

BOXES

THAT

SPEAK

CLEARLY

*T*he fundamental way by which Windows provides feedback and solicits input is via dialog boxes. Understanding good dialog-box design requires both an understanding of the kinds and uses of dialog boxes (which are discussed in this chapter) and of the usage and placement of controls (which are discussed in the next chapter.)

Characteristics of Dialog Boxes

Windows allows all kinds of dialog boxes. They can be differentiated by these characteristics:

- Whether they're *nonmodal, application modal, system modal,* or *application semimodal*
- Whether they're movable or fixed
- Whether they're message boxes or standard dialog boxes
- Whether they unfold or not

Dialog Box Modality

In the GUI world, we're accustomed to being able to run a number of programs all at the same time, clicking from one application window to another at *our* pace, not the pace of the application. But sometimes an application must demand our attention, refusing to do anything until we respond to it. Sometimes the entire *system* must wait for an answer. So different dialog boxes have different kinds of *modalities*. The name of each kind of modality defines what has to wait for the user to respond to the dialog box (nothing, the application in use, or the system).

An example of a more typical modeless dialog box is the Spelling dialog box displayed by Word for Windows, which allows the user to continue editing the document while the dialog box remains displayed on the screen. Toolbars may or may not be implemented as modeless dialog boxes.

Nonmodal Dialog Boxes

Nonmodal dialog boxes demand nothing of us; they merely inform or await input. A toolbar is an example of a nonmodal dialog box. It just sits on the screen and will respond to you when you click on it, but it won't burn up a single cycle of CPU time unless you click it.

Use nonmodal dialog boxes wherever possible.

Application Modal Dialog Boxes

Sometimes an application cannot proceed without advice from the user. For example, an error while printing like an "out of paper" message may not be one that the application can ignore easily. In another example, many applications do not let you edit a document while the application is printing the document; as a result, you get a dialog that says something like Figure 8.1 (at least from Ami Pro).

This is called an *application* modal dialog box because you can't do anything with Ami—even though it's an MDI application, you can't edit one document when printing another—while the dialog box is displayed but you *can* always Ctrl-Esc or Alt-Tab over to another application.

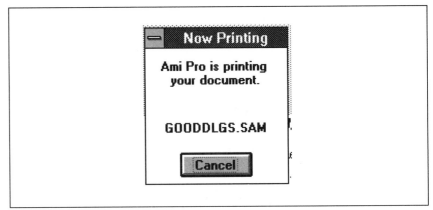

Event-driven programs should be as nonmodal as possible, but there are just times when the crush of events requires that the whole show stop until something is attended to. In other cases, as in the Ami print case, it's just programmer laziness. I don't mean to pick on Lotus here; virtually every Windows program does the same thing, unfortunately.

System Modal Dialog Boxes

Worst of all in the taxonomy of dialog boxes are the system modal dialogs. They usually mean plenty bad news.

A system modal dialog is one that stops the *whole system*—communications, processing, and all—until the user responds. Think you've never seen one? Sure you have—the General Protection Fault or Not Present error dialogs are system modal dialog boxes.

In general, applications should not be using system modals; that level of severity would be detected only by the operating system. And yet some applications (read on about Video for Windows) seem to think that any problem that *they* encounter is one that *you* had better drop everything and resolve, *now*. Personally, I'd say that this kind of solipsistic programming is far too reminiscent of mid-80's DOS programs for my taste.

Application Semimodal Dialog Boxes

Semimodal dialogs are procedural—that is, they appear because of an action that's being taken—but that can be ignored. The most common example is choosing a range within a spreadsheet. Some spreadsheets provide a dialog into which you can enter coordinates, then allow you to drag the mouse across the desired range.

Movable vs. Fixed dialogs

It is possible to specify that a dialog box cannot be moved. This is pretty unusual, however, and the only fixed-location dialogs that I can ever remember seeing are the GPF/Not Present error boxes.

Avoid fixed dialogs; don't constrain people any more than you have to. That doesn't mean that people haven't *used* them where they weren't needed, however. To see an example of something truly silly, fire up Microsoft's Video for Windows program. The first time that you run it with a new display driver, it does a small benchmark on the video board to see if it's fast enough for Video For Windows. It never is—either every video board on the planet is inadequate, or there's a bug in the benchmark's criteria—and so you get a dialog that says "Warning: You may encounter display performance problems, please contact the manufacturer of your video board to see if an updated driver is available." First, I can imagine how excited the makers of every video board in the world were to see *this* message. But even more amazingly, this dialog shuts down everything until you respond, because it's a *system modal, fixed dialog box*! This is the moral equivalent of the Scheduler program using a system modal fixed dialog to remind you to call Mom.

Unfolding Dialogs

Often a dialog box will contain details that could confuse users, options that are irrelevant the vast majority of the time. One way to shield your users from detail is with an *unfolding dialog box*. For example, consider the dialog box in Figure 8.2, also taken from Video for Windows.

F I G U R E **8.2**

An unfolding dialog box

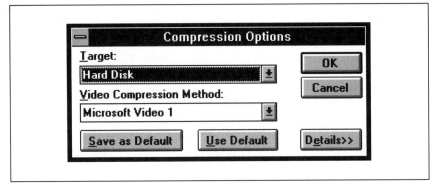

Notice the "Details>>" button. Click it, and the dialog box changes to look like Figure 8.3.

There is no special built-in support for folding dialogs in Windows; you just add a button which, if pressed, you respond to by erasing one kind of dialog box and displaying a different one.

FIGURE 8.3

The Details window from the unfolding dialog box

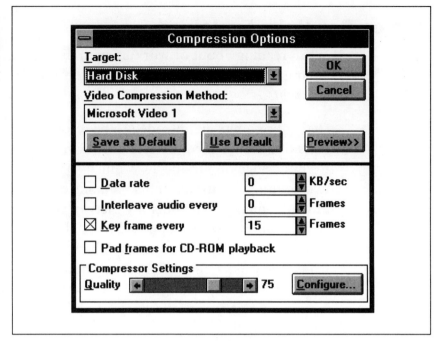

By the way, notice what this unfolded dialog box lacks: a way to fold it up again. Don't you make that mistake. People want to explore, and to be able to say, "Ahhh ... mebbe not"; the fact that there's no "hide details" button leads one to believe that he's in too deep to get out at this point.

Message Dialogs

While there's no technical difference between message dialog boxes (or message box) and other dialogs, their common use has set message boxes aside. A message dialog is an application or system modal dialog box.

Message dialogs are used for confirmation, warning, and information.

Dialog Box Units Explained

When reading about or working with dialog box design tools, a phrase comes up with a fair amount of frequency: *dialog box units.*

Dialog box units are intended to be resolution-independent units of distance used to describe how far items should be from the edge of a frame, how much space should sit between two command buttons, and so on. Since Windows is intended to work equally well under a variety of resolutions, and Windows *applications* are supposed to do the same, it wouldn't do to say that two buttons should be five pixels apart; that would look okay on a VGA screen, but cramped on an 8514 screen. That's why dialog boxes are supposed to be described in units that vary with the resolution of the screen—dialog box units (DBUs).

Your programs can get the value of a DBU for the particular screen that your system is running on with an API function called GetDialogBaseUnits. There is another function called MapDialogRect that will convert DBUs on the current system to pixels. Using DBUs as your measuring unit will help your dialog boxes to be proportional, no matter what resolution your application is seen at.

The size of a system's DBU is computed from the size of the default System font. A DBU's width equals one quarter the width of a character, and its height is one eighth of a character's height. As character box ratios are roughly 1:2, that implies that DBUs are roughly square.

DBUs are important because they are the way that you'd tell C or some other non-GUI development tool how large a dialog box should be and where to place it on the screen. For example, to place a check box in a dialog box in a non-GUI development tool like, in this case, the Resource Compiler, you'd use this command:

```
CHECKBOX "Message",id,x,y,width,height
```

Don't worry about the specifics of this except to see that *x* and *y* place the check box, and *width* and *height* describe the width and height of the check box—and all four of those values must be in DBUs.

Notice, however: **DBU size is not dependent on your screen resolution; it is dependent on your chosen system font size.**

If you're using C and the Software Development Kit (SDK) to build your Windows applications, then there's no problem here, as many of its tools work not in absolute numbers of pixels, but rather in the relative units of DBUs. But if you're using some kind of screen-builder product like Visual Basic, then you're potentially in trouble, as they typically don't work in DBUs. If that's the case, then use these rough rules of thumb:

- When using the "VGA" or "Small" fonts, the character box is 15 pixels high by 8 pixels wide, so a DBU is about 2 pixels each way.

- When using the "8514" or "Large" fonts, the character box is 20 pixels high by 10 wide, so a DBU is about 2.5 pixels wide.

Argghh... 2.5 pixels. Since in reality every item on the screen must lie on a pixel boundary, you've got to make a choice to either go with two pixels or three pixels. Now, many programmers make the choice to just use two pixels, because then they needn't change the dialog box according to system font.

That's not a bad choice, but remember always to *test your application with different fonts in different resolutions.* Some people load the 20×10 fonts when working with *VGA*, don't forget. A fair number of applications look terrible when run with the large fonts; clearly they've never been tested at higher resolutions.

Placing a Dialog Box

By default, a dialog box appears in the center of the application's window. That makes sense sometimes, but not always.

For example, consider a Find/Replace or Spell Check dialog box. These dialog boxes appear when a word that was searched for was found, or when a misspelled word is found. Placing the dialog in the center of the screen might obscure the user's view of the word in question. It could be a better choice to have such a dialog box usually appear in the center of the screen, but have it be flexible enough to move if it will conceal the selected word if it remains there.

Further, consider what the dialog box is concerned with. If it's allowing you to choose a color for an object, put the dialog near the object, as your user's attention is already drawn to that location. And consider remembering the *last* place that the user moved your dialog box to; if he pulled it over to the corner the last time that the box appeared, then perhaps it's a good idea to put it back in that location the next time that the box appears. If you do that, however, then check that the dialog box ends up in a visible location. It's quite possible that "in the corner" in 1024×768 mode is "off the screen" in 640×480—and, yes, a lot of people alternate between different resolutions in a normal work day.

Adding little touches like this to a program separate programs that feel "thought out" from the ones that are just the products of a loaded C compiler pointed in an unfortunate direction.

Laying Out Controls within a Dialog Box

A dialog box is really just a window that lacks a minimize/maximize option and sizing, and that contains a number of *controls*, objects that your user can control something with—buttons, text fields, slider bars, and the like.

You'll learn about those controls in the next chapter, but for now let's look at how to aesthetically arrange those controls.

When I say "aesthetically," I'm not being flip. When we use programs, we rely on the user interface to be consistent and not distracting. A poorly laid-out dialog box distracts a user from whatever it is she's trying to do. Therefore, keep these things in mind when you're designing the layout of dialog boxes.

- Button placement should assist in anticipating common usages and grouping of purposes.
- Buttons should all be arranged horizontally or vertically.

- Buttons should be large enough to accommodate command names entirely on their faces.

- The most commonly-chosen command button (often the OK button), which may be the most important button, should be all the way to the left for horizontally arranged buttons, and at the top for a column of buttons.

- The Help button should be at the opposite end of the row or column of buttons, with appropriate spacing.

- Dialog boxes should be reserved for pretty specific functions. Try to avoid putting more than three or four buttons in a dialog box, as in one including OK, Cancel, Network, and Help.

Placing Buttons Vertically

If you are going to use a dialog box with buttons arranged in a column (like the one below), follow these guidelines shown in Figure 8.4.

There are just a few things that you must do to create a dialog looking like this one:

- Make all buttons the same height and width. Fit a button to the largest command, and then make all of the other buttons that size.

- Make sure that the text fits on the button face, and doesn't curve down the sides, like in Figure 8.5.

FIGURE 8.4

A vertically arranged dialog box

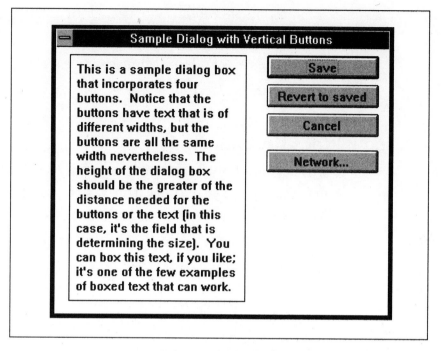

FIGURE 8.5

Arranging text on the button face

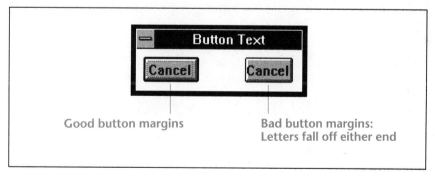

- Use the space between buttons to separate their function and group them. For example, Help should be separate from the command buttons.

  Leave 6 DBUs (Dialog Box Units, remember) margin to the top, bottom, left, and right.

> Leave 3 DBUs of white space between buttons in the same group.
>
> Leave 6 DBUs of white space between groups.

- OK and Cancel should be next to each other.

Placing Buttons Horizontally

If you've got buttons whose text length varies widely, you may choose to use buttons arrayed horizontally. The rules for horizontal buttons are:

- All button heights must be equal. Wide buttons with one line of text are better than buttons of differing heights with multiple lines of text. Buttons shouldn't have multiple lines of text on them, anyway; recast the message to make it no longer than two or three words.

- Button widths can vary.

- Leave 6 DBUs white space margin from the top, bottom, left, and right of the dialog box.

- Leave 4 DBUs white space between buttons within the same group.

- Leave 6 DBUs white space between buttons within different groups.

- Put OK and Cancel to the left part of the box.

Cancel Versus Stop

It's customary to offer some kind of visual indicator of progress, such as a moving bar, for anything that takes more than a second or two to accomplish. For example, consider the dialog shown in Figure 8.6.

FIGURE **8.6**

**Cancel button vs.
Stop button**

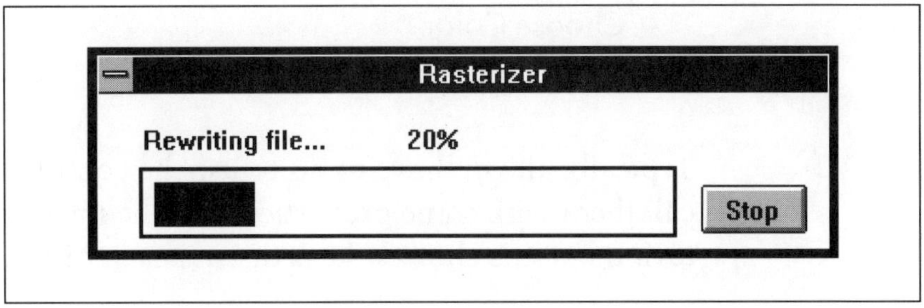

Notice that the button isn't labeled *Cancel*—it's labeled *Stop*. What's the difference? Well, in this case, a process is underway that can't be undone. Stopping this will not restore the file (whatever kind of file it was) to its previous state.

If it is at all possible to offer a Cancel rather than an Stop, then by all means do so. But if there's no way to restore things to their pre-action state, then use Stop.

Using the Common Dialog Boxes

Building dialog boxes is a pain. Spending hours measuring DBUs is not only frustrating, it also chews up time and may permanently derail your train of thought.

That's why it's nice that as of Windows 3.1, there are a set of "common" dialog boxes that come pre-built with the operating system. They include:

- File Open
- Save As
- Print
- Select Printer

- Choose Color
- Choose Font

Typically all you have to do to use the common dialogs is to call them with some properties, and then wait for them to return the user's choices. Let's discuss each of these in turn.

File Open Common Dialog Box

The File Open box will automatically handle these things for you:

- It will put a standard File Open dialog on the screen.
- You can include a "Read Only" check box if you want.
- You can specify a default extension.
- You can define items displayed in the "File type" pull-down.
- It will allow you to choose whether or not your user's allowed to pick multiple files.

For example, if I wanted to create a File Open dialog box that either allowed text files—which I define as files with the extension DOC or TXT—or bitmaps—which I define as files with the extension BMP or PCX—then this is all I'd have to do:

```
cmdialog1.Filename = ""
cmdialog1.Filter = "Text|*.txt;*.doc|Bitmaps
    |*.bmp;*.pcx"
cmdialog1.Action = 1
MsgBox cmdialog1.Filename
```

That's Visual BASIC, but doing it from C is just about as easy.

Note that the second line is broken; in actual usage, that would not occur.

File Save As Common Dialog Box

The Save As dialog does the same things as the Open dialog, with a few extra features:

- You can have it check to see if creating a file would over-write an existing file and put an "Are you sure?" message box up for confirmation.
- You can make it ignore file-sharing errors.

Fonts Dialog Box

The Fonts dialog will show available fonts and let your user choose one from the possible fonts:

- You can specify maximum and minimum size shown.
- You can only show printer fonts, or ignore printer fonts.
- The dialog box allows choosing font colors.
- You can choose to only show the character fonts, and ignore the symbol fonts.

The one drawback to using the Fonts dialog is that it's a bit unstable; getting it to see your fonts may be difficult from in-side Visual Basic.

Colors Dialog Box

The Colors dialog is similar to the one that you see when you choose Custom Colors in the Control Panel. It allows you to

mix your own colors, or choose from a prebuilt value set of colors.

- You can disable the ability to mix a color.
- You can restrict the colors returned to your application.

Print Dialog Box

The Print dialog has a variety of options:

- Which printer to use (including a Network button that will let you connect to printer resources on the network)
- Draft quality
- Range to print

A dialog with all these options appears just with a few lines of code. The Print Dialog is probably the most powerful of the common dialogs; get to know it and use it.

No one's saying that you *must* use the common dialogs. But using them has three great benefits. First, your application ends up looking like other Windows applications, which makes the user more comfortable and reduces the learning time for the application. Second, you save time writing your application. And third, your application's look and feel will automatically change with Windows. If some future version of Windows, say a Windows 4.0, has a different set of common dialogs, then your application will attach to them in any case with no extra programming.

Using Message Dialog Boxes

Something like a common dialog, message dialogs are the most common dialog box around. They are so common that some GUI design environments, like Visual Basic, have them as a predefined, built-in function. You needn't take the time to build a new window; you just add the line

```
MsgBox "My message",identifier,"Box Title"
```

where "My message" is whatever you want said in the box, "identifier" is a code indicating what type of box to show and what buttons to include, and "Box Title" is the string that goes on the title bar.

Providing Information

Probably the most common message box uses either an exclamation point or a question mark icon, as you see in Figures 8.7 and 8.8.

FIGURE 8.7

A message dialog box using the exclamation point

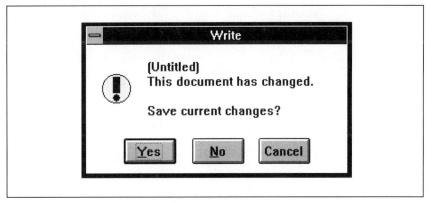

FIGURE **8.8**

A message dialog box using the question mark

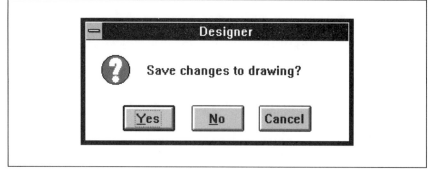

The exclamation point, as you see in Figure 8.7, is the currently preferred method (according to Microsoft), as the question mark is said to be associated with Help in some people's minds, and as a result would confuse those people. You see the question-mark version in Figure 8.8.

In actuality, you can probably get away with using either the question mark or the exclamation point.

Fatal and Critical Errors

Another dialog is the "stop sign" dialog, indicating some kind of critical or fatal error, as you see it used (incorrectly) in Figure 8.9.

FIGURE **8.9**

The Stop sign used (incorrectly) in an information dialog box

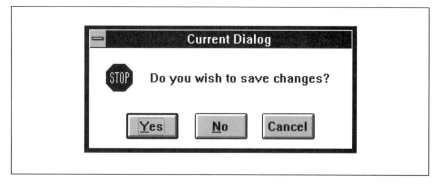

Use the Stop sign when some kind of hardware failure has made completing an operation impossible and irreversible or continuing on a current path would cause some important level of irreparable damage.

The keys to when to use this dialog are the words *irreparable* and *irreversible*. It should appear either when something bad has happened that can't be fixed, or when something bad *could* happen that can't be fixed. Use it sparingly.

Information

Another common kind of message box is the "information" dialog, which uses a lowercase *i* in an icon, and usually provides some kind of information (see Figure 8.10).

FIGURE **8.10**

An information dialog box

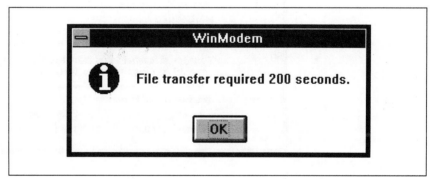

Use the information icon to indicate that a lengthy operation is finished. Usually the only button in an information dialog is an OK button. This is the classic example of the nonmodal dialog box. (Unfortunately, not everyone understands that— Visual Basic, for example, only offers application modal and system modal options for MsgBox. Oh well.)

Copyright and "About..." Message Dialogs

This isn't a standard system dialog, but one simple message box that you'll end up creating is an About... dialog box. You see the About... dialog from Windows 3.1's Program Manager in Figure 8.11.

F I G U R E **8.11**

An About...**dialog box**

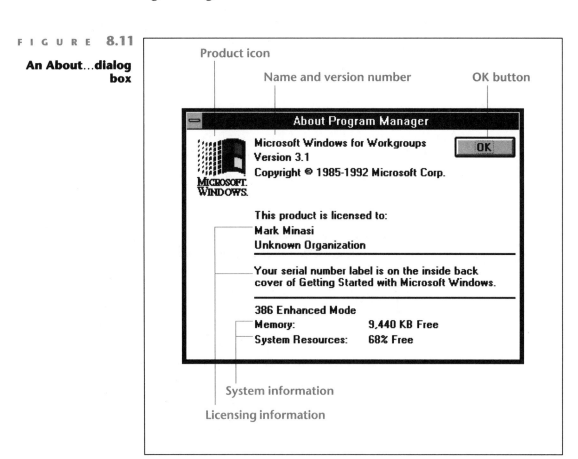

Again there *is* no prebuilt message box for this. But nearly every application has an About... box, and yours should also. It's unsettling to not find it. Place the About... box on the Help menu.

The About... box has become something of a showcase for programmer cleverness. Some About... boxes include hidden animations; the best-known is probably the Windows "gang screen" which rolls credits of everyone who worked on the Windows project. Word 2.0x for Windows has a short animation showing a number of happy users menaced by an evil WordPerfect monster, which is crushed to death by the Word for Windows logo; the users jump up and down and cheer, fireworks explode, and the credits for Word for Windows roll. Don't overdo it, but here's an opportunity for you to pat yourself on the back for a job well done.

Unhelpful Dialog Boxes

While we're discussing what to do to make your dialog boxes better, it's worthwhile to discuss what *not* to do as well. Just about everyone has a GUI "better dead" list; that list of applications that are all right in their ways but have a less than perfect interface.

While we've already discussed how to arrange your dialog boxes for the maximum esthetic quality, the biggest culprit in a bad GUI is ambiguity. People use GUI applications to make things easier; if they have to spend time figuring out exactly what a dialog box means or what it's referring to, the point of using a graphical application is somewhat lost.

For example, imagine that I'm shutting down Windows. I've got a number of applications minimized at the bottom of my screen. As each application shuts itself off, it closes its open files. At one point, I see the dialog box shown in Figure 8.12.

F I G U R E **8.12**

An ambiguous "Save?" dialog box

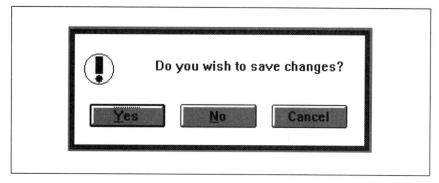

This dialog box tell me *nothing*: not the application name (although, in this case, I know which application this box corresponds to because, luckily, only one of my applications has this problem), not the file name to which the application refers, not anything useful. Like many other Windows applications, this particular one has the capability to support numerous open files. How, from this dialog box, can I tell which file of the five I had open this box refers to? It could be the throwaway file I'd started and then abandoned, or it could be the new company logo that I'd spent an hour editing.

A better example of the same type of dialog looks like Figure 8.13.

F I G U R E **8.13**

An unambiguous "Save?" dialog box

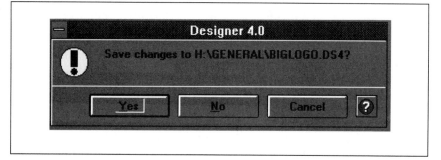

As you can see, this dialog box contains all the pertinent information that I need to answer the question. It tells you the name of the application that it refers to, and of the file currently open and unsaved in that application. The example here shows a previously named file that I had been editing, but had the file been new, the dialog box would have called the file "Untitled" or "Untitled 2" or whatever, depending on how many unnamed files I had open in that application. I rarely have more than two new files open at once, so it's easy for me to remember which *particular* unnamed file the dialog box refers to.

The moral here? Make sure that your applications dialog boxes contain enough information for the user to intelligently use them.

Another example of an unhelpful (and, in fact, downright dangerous) dialog box can be found in another graphics program. In this application, you have a variety of color maps to choose from in order to change the colors in your picture. You can also write new color maps and save them.

This is a good idea, and potentially quite useful, but in this application the dialog boxes for reading and writing color maps are identical to each other. From the dialog box, there is no way that you can tell if you're accessing a default color map or writing a new one to the name of a default. Not only that, but you access the dialog boxes from juxtaposing items in a drop-down menu, so one slip of the mouse gets you the wrong box and you'll never know it. My friend Maeve, who owns this application, accidentally corrupted a number of her default color maps before realizing the danger. (And, as she pointed out, with color maps being corrupted, can the rest of the country be far behind?)

The moral here is twofold:

- Title your dialog boxes, so people can tell what exactly the box is meant for.

- When a user saves new information to a filename that's in use (and is not currently open), the user should then see *another* dialog box informing her that that filename is in use and asking her if it's okay to overwrite that file. This may take an extra mouse-click to save a file, but it can prevent the user from overwriting files that she didn't intend to.

What, exactly, makes for a "bad" dialog box? Well, there's the story that I just told you, but here are some other examples of less-than-useful dialog boxes.

- There is a fad nowadays to use black text in dialog boxes, and medium gray backgrounds. This is a bad idea from the point of view of visibility; the contrast is poor.

- If an option is important, don't bury it in a dialog box that's kicked off by a button in a dialog box. It's far too difficult to find when needed later.

- Double-check the dialog boxes for different resolutions. Too many dialogs get clipped in 1024 × 768 resolution.

- Don't use bitmaps in dialog boxes; they make things too busy. Just stick to buttons, radio buttons, edit fields, and the like. And remember that many people are using monochrome laptops to run Windows; don't build a program that looks terrible on an LCD screen.

My final bit of advice is the one that I've given before, and that I'll give again: Get some outside help. GUI programming is entirely about, and *only* about, usability. If you designed the program, then you are the single worst person on the planet to test it. Enlist testers, and *listen* to them.

UNDERSTANDING

AND

USING

CONTROLS

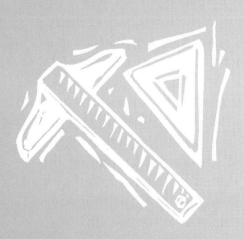

*T*he heart of your user's ability to interact with your program lies in objects on the screen called *controls*. Back before GUIs, the sole control was a text input field, a rectangular area that accepted text and, if well-designed, that monitored the text as it was being entered to check it for validity. GUIs bring many kinds of controls to the user interface arena. These varied controls attempt to make working with the user interface more familiar, closer metaphorically to already-known user interfaces like doors, automotive dashboards, TVs, VCRs, and other household appliances.

In this chapter, you'll be introduced to the common GUI controls and you'll learn how to use them properly.

Buttons

The most basic of all GUI controls, buttons are graphical controls that can indicate possible actions open to the user or can change the interface itself. Users can select a button either by clicking on it with the mouse, or with the keyboard, using either mnemonic access characters (such as Alt-H for Help) or keyboard shortcuts (such as X for Cancel or Ctrl-B for Bold), and if a button is in a Windows dialog box, users can use Tab or Shift-Tab to move the input focus to the button and then press the spacebar to "click" it. 3-D buttons should appear depressed so long as their option is selected (for example, if text is italicized, the Italic button should remain depressed so long as the cursor is on that text). If you use standard Windows buttons, then the 3-D effect will occur automatically.

Command Buttons and Option Buttons

There are two types of buttons: command buttons and option buttons. Each of them is appropriate to a certain situation.

In general, a command button makes something happen, *now*. Clicking an OK button makes something take effect. Clicking an option button, in contrast, usually sets some characteristic of the system. That characteristic may well involve an immediate action as a side-effect.

Command Buttons

Basically, a command button is a rectangular box with a label that specifies what the button does. The user selects a command by clicking on the button with the mouse or keyboard, as described above. When a button has the input focus, a black line will outline it. If the function of the button changes, the label of the button should change too.

For example, if the user performs an action in a dialog box that cannot be canceled, the Cancel button should change to Close to indicate that the Cancel option no longer exists.

Command buttons usually come in groups, such as Open and Cancel. You can specify one button to be the default (indicated by a black line around it) to be selected if the user presses ↵. You do that usually when defining the control.

Only one command button may be selected at a time.

There are several types of command buttons:

- **Action buttons.** Initiate an action from that dialog box. The usual ones are OK, Cancel, Close.

- **Jump buttons.** Close the current dialog box and open a new one. For example, a jump button could send the user to a second dialog box with more details about the available options in the first one.

- **Jump and Return buttons.** Open a new dialog box but do not close the old one. A Details… box could work like this.

- **Unfold buttons.** Expand the current dialog box to show more options. A possible example would be a Network… button.

- **Fold buttons.** Refold a dialog box.

Option Buttons/Radio Buttons

As their name suggests, option buttons present different possibilities to the user. As always, the trick to options is to offer enough options, but not too many.

Typically, each option button represents a single choice in a set of mutually exclusive choices. For example, in any group of radio buttons, the user can only select one at a time. Only one option can be selected but at least one option must be selected.

Because you don't want to offer *too* many options, only use radio buttons if you've got two to five options. If there are more than four options in your group, you can use standard or drop-down lists to save space, but radio buttons are preferable because they make the options more accessible to the user than the lists do.

There are two types of radio buttons:

- traditional radio buttons
- value sets

Traditional Radio Buttons

Traditional radio buttons are represented by circles: if the radio button's circle is filled, the option associated with that radio button is selected; if empty, the option is deselected. This type of radio button works well for options too long or too textual to work as a *value set*, a control you'll see soon.

Figure 9.1 shows an example of what command buttons and radio buttons look like in combination.

As you can see, the OK button is the default (it's got the black line around it) and the other buttons are ordinary command buttons. In this picture, none of the radio buttons are currently selected. When they are the default, they are surrounded by a dotted rectangle. When a radio button has the

F I G U R E **9.1**

Sample command buttons and radio buttons

input focus, a dotted line is drawn around it; in this case, the user can check it using the space bar (the focus is moved from button to button with Tab or Shift-Tab). Also, as in Figure 9.1, when a program first displays a dialog box, it usually selects one of the radio buttons in each group (indicating the current or default choice), least because at one button must be selected.

It is customary to surround groups of radio buttons with a *group* rectangle, discussed later.

Value Sets

A value set is a group of adjacent rectangular buttons that contain their labels within the button, either as a graphic or as text. This type of radio button works well for options best represented by graphics (such as drawing tools or colors) or with labels short enough to fit within a small rectangle. Figure 9.2 shows a sample value set.

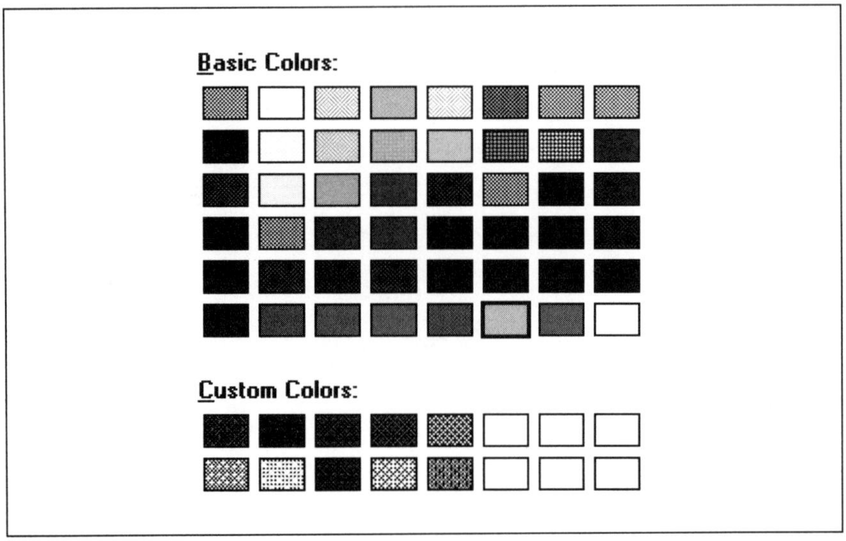

FIGURE 9.2

A sample value set

One thing to be aware of when using value sets and radio buttons is that the whole process of selecting one and only one option is something that you, the programmer, must typically take care of. Not only must you define them, you've also got to deselect the other buttons when a new button is selected—the user interface (Windows, in this case) doesn't do it for you.

The best strategy in Visual Basic is to make all related radio buttons into an array. Then you can handle them all with a single loop command, disabling all of the radio buttons but the one that was just clicked.

Check Boxes

Unlike radio buttons, the user can select more than one check box at a time. You'll use these boxes when the user needs to choose from a series of options that needn't be mutually exclusive.

A dialog box containing several check boxes would look like Figure 9.3.

FIGURE **9.3**

Check boxes

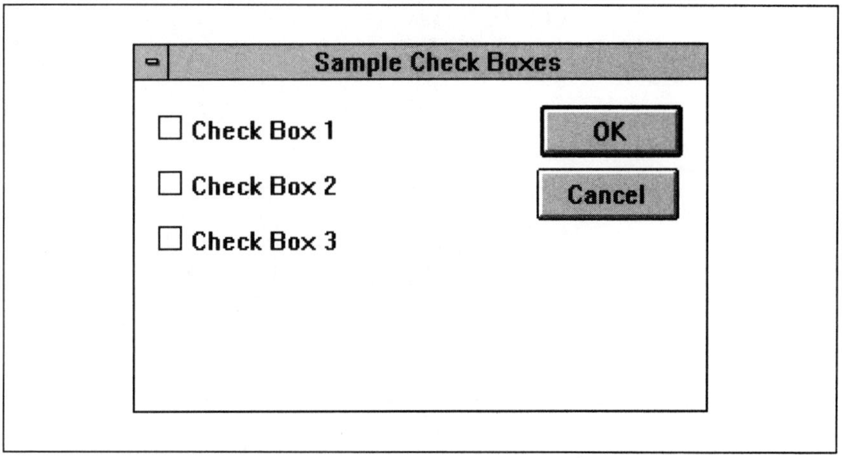

Sample Check Boxes

☐ Check Box 1

☐ Check Box 2

☐ Check Box 3

OK

Cancel

Check boxes control individual choices that can be turned on or off. When off, the option's box is blank; when on, the option's box has an X in it. It's not necessary to have any of the check boxes enabled at all—none of the boxes need be enabled. The user can select more than one choice or *no* choices.

Using Check Boxes

You'll find check boxes useful for a number of things. Here are a few suggestions:

- You can group check boxes, but don't prevent the user from turning the boxes on and off in any combination. If desirable, you can create a check box that allows the user to select all options at once.

- You can use check boxes to set properties of a selection. If the selection is heterogeneous, all check boxes should be filled with a gray pattern. If you click a grayed check box once, it should get an X in it to turn on the selection, and if you click it again, the box should go blank, deselecting that option. Clicking it a third time will return the box to its original gray. You can see an example of this in Figure 9.4.

- You *can* use radio buttons or drop-down lists in place of checkboxes, but it's generally not a good idea. If you use check boxes, you'll need to include a "normal" or "none" box to allow the user to indicate that none of the options should be selected. If you use drop-down lists, not only will you need the extra "normal" option, but most of the options will be hidden.

Placing Check Boxes

Check box placement is pretty much the same as other controls, as was covered in the last chapter. Before leaving the subject of check boxes, however, notice that all the labels for the check boxes in the previous figure appear to the immediate right of the check box, and that there's a margin of about 6 DBUs to the left of the check boxes. The right margin in this example is probably a bit too large; it should be about 6 DBUs to the right of the last character in "Line position."

List Boxes

List boxes are used to display choices, represented by text, color or graphics, for the user. There are several kinds of list boxes:

Standard single-selection list box. All available options are displayed and the user can only select one of them. Example: the File area in File Open.

Drop-down single-selection. Available options are only displayed when the user clicks on the drop-down arrow. Example: the wallpaper selections in the Desktop section of the Windows Control Panel.

Standard multiple-selection. All available options are displayed; the user can select more than one. Example: the Windows File Manager.

Drop-down multiple-selection. Options are only displayed when the user activates the drop-down menu; the user can make more than one selection with the usual Ctrl-click and Shift-click.

Using List Boxes

As I mentioned earlier, you handle list boxes much as you'd expect from the discussion of keyboard handling. Here are the details:

- You can use either the mouse or the up- and down-arrow keys to move the highlighted area to another selection. Selected choices are highlighted.

- If a choice is not available for the currently selected thing (if, for example, a particular point size is not available for the selected font) you should remove that choice from the list box. Notice the difference from menus, where items should never be removed.

- If you need to indicate that the choice exists but it's not available right now, you can just dim the choice. If an entire list box is unavailable, dim its heading.

- As a shortcut to selecting the desired item and then choosing the default command button in a dialog box, you can double-click on an item in a single-selection list.

Operating List Boxes

Drop-down lists can be toggled between the closed and open states by:

- Clicking on the drop-down arrow
- Pressing Alt+↑
- Pressing Alt+↓
- Pressing ↵ or clicking on the field at the top of the list.

When a list has the focus and is closed, pressing ↓ opens it. Scrolling is permitted only when a list is open. Any new item selection made while the list is open is accepted and displayed in the list field. The change is not made, however, until the user presses OK and closes the dialog box.

An open drop-down list can be closed by:

- Pressing Alt+↑
- Pressing Alt+↓
- Tab or other navigation method
- Pressing ↵ (which does not close the dialog).

Comparing Standard List Boxes to Drop-Down List Boxes

Standard list boxes and drop-down list boxes are very similar; the only difference is in how they look. Standard list boxes show from three to eight choices in a complete list that the user can see at all times, while drop-down lists show only the first item of their three to eight options. (Each kind of list can, technically, have more options, but more than eight options or so can get confusing.)

Figure 9.5 shows two standard single-selection list boxes.

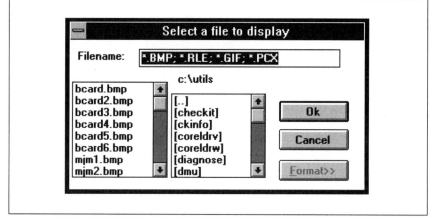

There are actually two list boxes in this dialog box—the one on the left with **bcard.bmp** as the first entry, and the one on the right with [..] at its top.

You can see three drop-down single-selection list boxes in the dialog box shown in Figure 9.6.

If you were to click one of the pull-down buttons to the right of any one of the three drop-down list boxes, then you'd see the options that the list box offers. You can only display one drop-down list at a time.

List Boxes Details

The next sections provide details on each kind of list box.

Standard List Boxes

- Display the entire list (three to eight items) at once.

- If the choices in a list represent possible attribute values for a selection, the current value should be selected when the list is first displayed. If the selection is heterogeneous, no value should be selected.

- When space is limited, standard lists may be replaced by drop-down lists. You see a standard list in Figure 9.7.

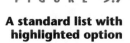

FIGURE 9.7

A standard list with highlighted option

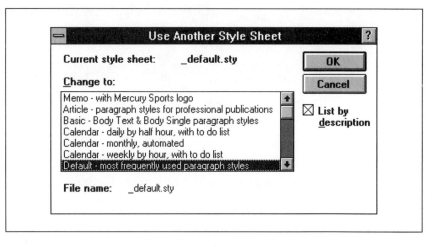

Drop-Down List Boxes

- Until clicked upon, displays only the current selection of a list of three to eight options.

- If a drop-down list contains more than eight items, it should have a scroll bar on the side.

- When a drop-down list is open, the list extends to the right edge of the drop-down arrow button, to allow the user to drag into the list.

- If the choices in a drop-down list represent possible attribute values for a selection, and the selection is varied, the user should see no value when the list is closed, and no value should be selected when the list is open. You see a dropped-down list box in Figure 9.8.

FIGURE **9.8**

A drop-down list box when open

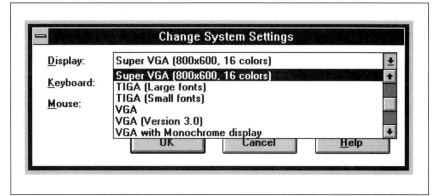

Notice the scroll bar on the side of the drop-down list. It's there because the list has more than eight options, and, rather than display the entire long list, you'll generally have the user scroll down the list.

Single-Selection, Multiple-Selection, and Extended Lists

Different situations demand different selection possibilities. Sometimes, your users will only want to make one selection from a list, sometimes, more than one adjoining selection, and sometimes a variety of selections that are not listed consecutively.

Single-selection list boxes work much like radio buttons, in that you can only make one selection from a series of options, and you must choose one of the proffered selections (or exit that dialog box).

Although list boxes are similar to radio buttons in function, you should use list boxes rather than radio buttons if you have more than four options, the size and composition of the choices varies considerably or if the layout of the dialog box requires it.

If the user presses a character key while the focus is on a single-selection list box, the list scrolls to the first item that begins with that character (if there are any such items), and highlights that item. If there is no matching item on the list, the list does not scroll and the highlight remains where it was.

Multiple-selection boxes are similar to check boxes in function, except that they may have more than four choices.

Multiple-selection boxes are useful when users may want to select several entries from a list but the entries are not grouped in a way that makes extended selection useful (see below). In fact, they are designed for selecting a number of items not necessarily next to each other. You should probably precede each item in the list with a check box for selecting.

This is *not* a predefined Windows control. You've got to do a lot of programming to get this to work.

Extended selection is designed for the times when a user wants to apply an action to more than one target at a time (for example, using the File Manager to copy more than one file). Contiguous list entries are related in a way meaningful to the user, such as by date, by file type, or in some other way.

Extended-selection lists should support the mouse and keyboard techniques for contiguous and disjoint selections.

▶ Shift-F8 turns on Add mode, which allows user to move the focus indicator (the dotted box) independently of the selection highlight.

▶ The spacebar toggles the selection state of the item that has the focus and sets a new anchor point there, without deselecting other items.

▶ Shift-Navigation or Shift-click propagates the selection state of the item at the current anchor point.

When no modifier keys or special modes are in effect, extended-selection lists behave just like single-selection lists.

Text Boxes

Text boxes are edit controls into which the user types information. The user can accept the current text, edit it, delete it, or replace it. In Figure 9.9, the File name and Document description fields are text fields.

FIGURE **9.9**

A text box

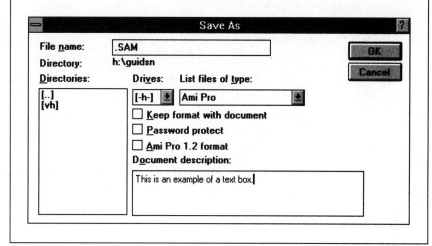

Characteristics of Text Boxes

Here are the details on text boxes.

- Most text boxes are only one line tall, but applications may also use multiline edit controls such as the Document Description box shown above.

- In multiline edit controls, data too long to fit on one line may either wrap to the next or extend beyond the right-hand boundary of the control.

- Both single- and multiline text boxes should support automatic keyboard and mouse scrolling, to allow hidden data to be brought into view. Multiline edit controls may also include scroll bars.

Navigating in a Text Box

- The left and right arrow keys move the insertion point within the text in an text box; when combined with Ctrl, the same keys move the insertion point to the beginning and end of the text.

- Mouse and keyboard selection of text within edit controls follows the standard methods.

- To insert a carriage return in a multiline edit control in a dialog, the user must usually press Ctrl-↵, because ↵ alone will perform its usual function of choosing the default button and closing the dialog if there is a default button in the program's focus window. If not, then ↵ just inserts a carriage return into the edit control.

Pop-Up Text Fields

When it comes to displaying interface text, you're often cramped for space. Long pathnames may not fit into a file dialog, or, in Help text, you discover that you can't include inline definitions for every term. In such situations, you can use the read-only pop-up text field (generally indicated as green text) in your applications.

There are two kinds of pop-up text fields: open and closed.

- Open: opens a pop-up explanatory window without closing the original

- Closed: closes the original window before opening the pop-up

To open the pop-up window:

> **With the mouse.** The user positions the cursor near the green underlined text. When the cursor changes to a hand, the user can click the number 1 mouse button to open the pop-up window. To close the pop-up window, the user clicks anywhere outside the window. Closing the pop-up does not affect the original window.
>
> **With the keyboard.** The user can navigate to the text field with T. If the field is labeled (as it should be unless it appears in a continuous stream of text), the user can also use the mnemonic contained in the field label (the underlined letter of the field label) with Alt to navigate to the field. To open and close the popup, the user can press the spacebar or any of the keys used for opening and closing drop-down controls.

When the popup opens, its top left corner appears at the same position as the top-left corner of the original text. If the contents of the popup can change between invocations, the popup should be dynamically sized so that it is large enough to hold its current contents.

Sliders

You'll use sliders to display and adjust values on continuous dimensions such as pitch, color, volume, and brightness. A slider consists of a bar containing notches or measurement markings, plus an indicator perpendicular to the bar. The indicator shows the present value and can be dragged along the bar with the mouse to set a new value.

A slider may include a box that explicitly shows the slider's value, but that's not necessary, as you see in Figure 9.10.

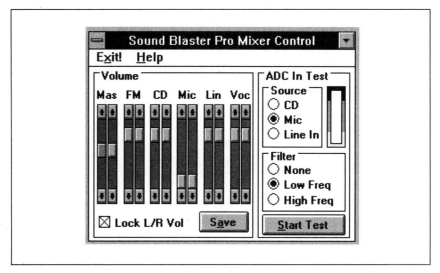

Static Text Fields

Static text fields are used to present text that will be read, but not altered, such as an error message or an informational message. These fields are called "static" because the user cannot change the text in them. The *application*, however, *can* alter the text to reflect the current state of the application. You can use static text fields to label controls for which the system does not automatically provide a label. The windows that you saw in Chapter 7 were displaying static text.

If a user tries to access a static text field with the keyboard (by pressing Tab or an arrow key), then Windows skips over the static text field, moving the focus to the next control in the Tab order. That's important because it suggests that when you use a static text field as a label, then you should put the control directly after the label in tab order. That way, tabbing over to a label gets the user to the control next to the label—which is probably what he wanted anyway.

Group Boxes

A group box is a rectangular one-pixel frame with a label in its upper-left corner, such as you see in Figure 9.11.

FIGURE 9.11

A group box

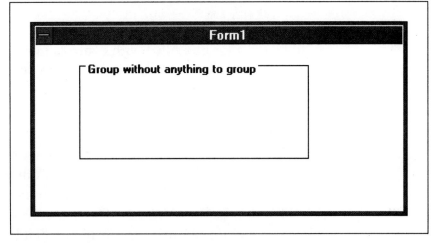

Group boxes are *technically* considered controls by Microsoft, but they really do not process any mouse or keyboard input; they simply let you group together controls that are logically related. They let you provide the user with a visual association of related controls by drawing a box around them and labeling it. You can see a real-world group box in Figure 9.12.

Find & Replace Options   **?**

┌─ Find Options ─────┐
☒ Whole word only
☐ Exact case
☐ Exact attributes

┌─ Replace Options ──┐
☐ Exact case
☐ Exact attributes

Range & direction:
☐ Beginning of document
☒ Include other text streams
☐ Find backwards

Find & replace type:
◉ Text
○ Style

OK

Cancel

Group boxes are a good way to "cheat" and reduce what could be a dialog box filled with controls into an easy-to-read, well-organized tool for controlling an application.

Combo Boxes

A combo box is something of a combination of an editable text field and a list box (see Figure 9.13). Combo boxes are useful when the application requires user input and can display a list of possible responses. The user can type a response in the text box if the correct one is not available in the list. That's how a combo box is different from a list box: with a list box, your only choices are the items on the list. On a combo box, you can type in an entirely new item if you like, one not already on the list.

Like list boxes, combo boxes can be classified into two categories (standard and drop-down), according to which type of list they include.

FIGURE **9.13**

A combo box

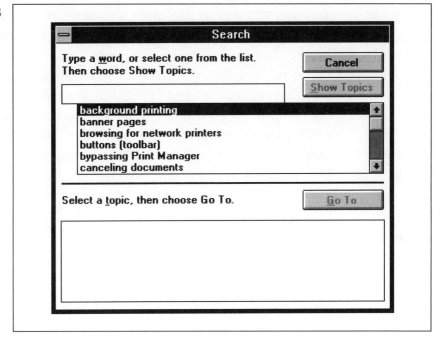

This is an interesting combo box in that, as you type information into the edit field part, the highlight goes to the closest match for that item in the Topics list. This is a useful function that can save a lot of time while doing searches.

Spinners

A spinner consists of a text box with a pair of arrows (an upward-pointing arrow above a downward-pointing arrow) attached to the right side of the box. Although they look like controls, spinners are actually specialized text boxes that only accept a limited set of discrete, ordered input values.

The user can manipulate the value in the text box in one of three ways: by typing a new value into the text box; by clicking the ↑ to increase the value; or by clicking the ↓ to decrease the value. In effect, the arrows function like scroll arrows for a hidden list that is sorted in descending order (in contrast to normal list controls, where entries are normally sorted in ascending order). Notice how spinners are different from sliders—there is a text field that you can type directly into on a spinner; there isn't one on a slider.

Spinners can be used to display values that consist of several subcomponents (e.g. times, which consist of hours, minutes and seconds). In such cases, the text box is divided into several subfields, and the subfields are separated by suitable separators (e.g. in the U.S., : for times or / for dates). The arrows affect the selected subfield; if no subfield is selected; the arrows affect the subfield representing the smallest unit of measurement. The spinners in Figure 9.14 are used to select the beginning and ending times for an appointment.

A value typed into the text field of a spinner should be validated either immediately or as soon as the user navigates away from the spin box. For example, if the user types a letter into a spin box that is only meant to accept numeric values (e.g., for dates), the application can beep (or alert the user in some other appropriate way) and either remove or simply never display the letter. Optionally, the value can be validated when the user presses OK to close the dialog box. At the time, if the value is invalid, the application should display an appropriate error message in a message dialog that contains a single OK button. Choosing OK to acknowledge the message should close the message dialog, but leave the original dialog open so that the user can change the invalid value.

F I G U R E   **9.14**

**Spinners used to
select time**

Control Labels

By now, you should have a pretty good idea of the various controls in dialog boxes and how they're used. The only things left to discuss before moving onto the next chapter are labeling and positioning conventions. After all, if you want your applications to be easy to use, users shouldn't have to spend time figuring out your particular labeling and positioning techniques. Better to expend creativity on the application itself.

Labels identify the function of each control and provide a means of direct keyboard access to it. Buttons, check boxes, and group boxes are automatically supplied with labels by the system, but you can label other controls with static text fields.

For the sake of consistency, you should follow the guidelines below:

1. Capitalize the initial letters of all words in control labels, except for articles (such as *a*, *an*, and *the*), conjunctions (such as *and*, *or*, *nor*, and *for*), prepositions (such as *by*, *through*, and *with*), and the infinitive form of verbs.

2. Provide a unique access character for labels of controls to which the user needs direct keyboard access. If possible, use the first character of the label as the access character. Use another letter from the label if:

   ▸ Another letter is more distinctive to that word (for example, the letter X in Exit).

   ▸ The label contains multiple words, one of which is more significant than the first word (for example, "Process" in Set Process).

   ▸ The first character has already been used as a access character for some other control.

3. Consonants make better access characters than vowels, because consonants are usually more distinctive and more easily remembered. Do not assign mnemonics to the OK button because it can be accessed through the ↵ key.

4. Dim the labels of unavailable or inapplicable controls.

5. Use a bold font so that dimming labels does not render them illegible.

6. Position controls as shown below.

CONTROL	LABEL POSITION
Command Button	Inside the button
Check box or option button	To right of box or button
Text box, spinner, list, combo box, slider, read-only popup text field	Above or to left of control, followed by colon, and left-aligned with the section of the dialog in which it appears
Group box	On top of (and replacing) part of top frame line, starting just after upper left corner

If some of those suggestions sound familiar, then that's because you've heard them before about using text in general, elsewhere in this book.

CHAPTER 10

MAKING

SURE

HELP

IS

NEVER

FAR

N o matter how well-written your application is, sooner or later a user will need help in operating it. Therefore, you need to put some thought to the question of your help file's design. Luckily, this isn't generally difficult, as most modern GUIs have some kind of help "engine" built right in, a program that accepts files that are a bit more than just the typical README.TXT stuff. These files typically support built-in "hypertext" links.

- Hypertext consists of words inside the displayed text that are a different color, or are highlighted; clicking on them jumps you to an other entry.

- Hypertext systems usually includes a "thread" control, a memory of where you've already been. This way, if you click on the wrong word and go in a direction that you didn't intend, there's always a way back.

The Windows Help Engine

The icon for any Windows help file typically looks like that shown in Figure 10.1.

FIGURE 10.1

The Windows Help Icon

Named WINHELP.EXE, the Help engine is associated with files with the extension HLP. Help files must be "compiled" with the Windows Help Compiler, but the original help file is created with a document processor that supports RTF (Rich Text Format). The Help compiler supports built-in text compression. The hardest part is in building the RTF format file— but I'll present a public-domain program that can do that job for you without any other software required.

Designing a Help File

Help-file construction can be frightening; virtually every reference to building Help under Windows tells you to first read the Help Compiler documentation included with the Help Compiler.

That's kind of a very nice way to say "Take a hike." Unfortunately, the Help Compiler documentation isn't all that good. Despite that, however, help construction isn't too bad a job, once someone explains it. Here's the overview on Help files under Windows.

Help Compiler "Topics"

Notice that Help screens are, in general, no more than a screen in size. Each of those screens in the Help Compiler is called a topic. It doesn't matter whether it's a full screen that pops up when you click on its reference, or a pop-up like the one shown in Figure 10.2.

That definition of a scroll bar is a topic, just as is the File Menu Commands screen that you see behind it.

FIGURE **10.2**

**A pop-up
Help screen**

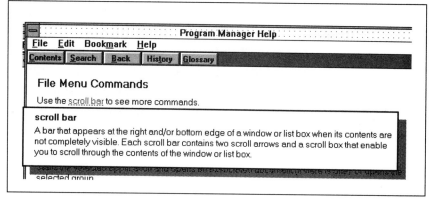

The First Topic: the Contents Topic

The very first topic is always called the "Contents" topic. It is a topic like any other, save that the Help Compiler is directed (by you) to make it the Contents topic. This topic serves as a directory of all the information in the Help file.

Linking Topics

The whole idea when building a Help file is to:

- Identify topics. Each topic should fit on about one screen.

- Define a Contents topic. It's important because it's the one that the Help engine will send the users to first.

- Because your help should be context-sensitive, there should be a help topic for each menu item on your program, as there should be for each submenu item and each control on every dialog box.

Eventually these files will have to be saved in a file format known as Rich Text Format (RTF), so be sure that your word processor knows how to convert to and from RTF. Word Perfect, Ami Pro, and Word for Windows all support RTF. Even if you don't have one of those word processors, you can create help files with an ASCII text editor like the Notepad if you use a public-domain program called RTFGEN, which I'll show you a bit later in this chapter. There are some tools around that use Word for Windows to create RTF-able files, but I haven't found them to be to my taste.

Help construction is easiest to explain with an example. I'll build a very simple help system about dinosaurs. It'll be just an explanation of the two major kinds of dinosaurs—the sauriscian, or "lizard-hipped" dinosaurs, and the ornithiscian, or "bird-hipped" dinosaurs. To start off, we'd probably have just three topics:

- Contents
- Sauriscians
- Ornithiscians

The next step would be to order them in some fashion. The simplest approach would probably be as you see in Figure 10.3.

Now, in order for your user to be able to even see the two other topics besides the Contents topic, there must be "Jump" references to the topics. Jumps are essential; without them, you "can't get there from here." The Help system originally places you in the Contents screen, but only via a jump can you get to the other topics. Jump phrases are usually represented in green, although you can define any jump color that you like.

FIGURE **10.3**

**A logical ordering
of the Help file**

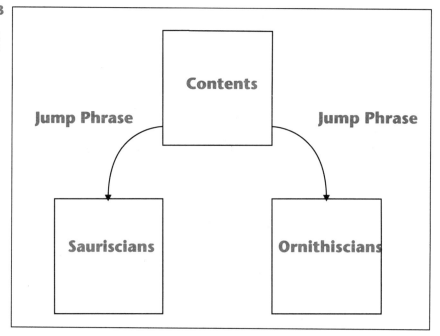

Creating a Help File: An Example

There's not time in this book, nor is it this book's intention, to show you how to build intricate help files. But it's easier to understand what help files are all about if you've built one, so I'll show you how to build a simple help file with a public domain tool called RTFGEN.

RTFGEN converts ASCII files that have been formatted in a particular way into RTF files, so that the files can be fed into Windows Help Compiler.

RTFGEN is the product of the hard work of a fellow named Dave Baldwin. Dave is on CompuServe at ID 76327,53, and keeps the two physical addresses shown on the next page.

(Summer)
22 Fox Den Rd.
Hollis, NH 03049
(603) 465-7857

(Winter)
144 13th St. East
Tierra Verde, FL 33715
(813) 867-3030

I found RTFGEN on the WINADV forum of CompuServe.

I'll build the help file discussed earlier, with three main topics: About Dinosaurs, Sauriscians, and Ornithiscians. I'll also include two other topics, a pop-up text topic and a bitmap topic.

What the Help File Should Look Like

The initial topic is the Contents topic and looks like Figure 10.4.

Again, notice the underlined words in the topic text. If the word has a normal underline, as you see here, clicking on that word (which will generally be shown in green) will send

FIGURE **10.4**

The Contents topic in the Help file

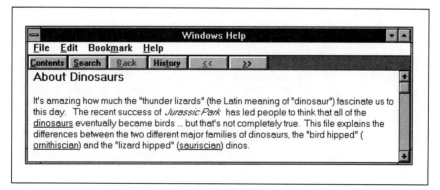

you to another topic. If the underline is dotted (as in the first instance of the word "dinosaurs") and the word is clicked, then this pop-up will appear, as you see in Figure 10.5.

There's also a "sauriscian" topic, which looks the screen shown in Figure 10.6.

F I G U R E **10.5**

The "Dinosaurs" definitional pop-up window

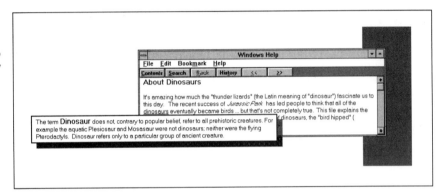

F I G U R E **10.6**

The "Sauriscians" jump window

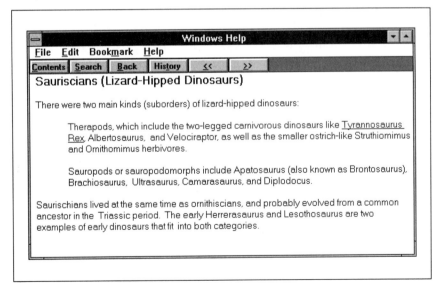

Notice the dotted underline for "Tyrannosaurus Rex"; I'd attach a bitmap there, although I won't display it here. Finally, the "Ornithiscian" topic would round out the help file; it would look like the window in Figure 10.7.

FIGURE **10.7**

The "Ornithiscians" jump window

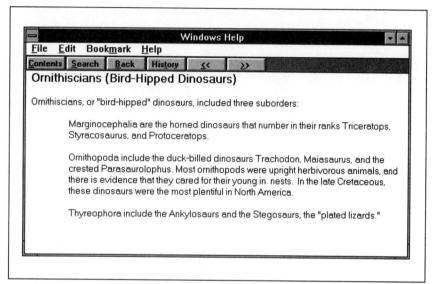

Writing the Help File in RTFGEN Format

Let's dig in and start writing this. First, some ground rules for writing things with RTFGEN. First, all commands start off with a \ and end off with an '. The very first command, which should sit on a line all its own, is **\docstart'**.

Topics are set off with a \topic line. The file with just the first topic would look like this:

```
\docstart'

\topic About_Dinosaurs'
\keyword introduction'
```

```
\keyword contents'
\keyword overview'
\title About Dinosaurs'
\browse General'
=========================
\b\fs24 About Dinosaurs'
It's amazing how much the "thunder lizards" (the
Latin meaning of "dinosaur") fascinate us to this
day.
The recent success of {\iJurassic Park} has led
people to think that all of the [[dino-
saurs:ddef]] eventually became birds ... but
that's not completely true. This file explains
the differences between the two different major
families of dinosaurs, the "bird hipped" ([orni-
thiscian:Ornithiscians]) and the "lizard hipped"
([sauriscian:Sauriscians]) dinos.'
-----------------------
```

The first line is **\topic About_Dinosaurs'**; that command just says that a topic is beginning, and its name is "About_Dinosaurs." This is not the name that appears anywhere in the help file; it's an internal topic name, which is the reason for the underscore—topic names can't have blanks in them.

The next three lines start off with **\keyword;** they define which keywords are listed when someone uses Search to find information. This topic will show up if you search "introduction," "contents," or "overview." Different keywords require different keyword lines. Again, each command starts with a \ and ends with an ' apostrophe.

The **\title** command is actually quite unimportant; it only shows up when you use the History option on Help. **\browse General** allows a user to see this by clicking the Next button on the Help window.

The first few commands are what might be called the "header" of the topic. The actual topic text is separated from the header by a line of equals signs. Then, whatever text appears is the topic's text, until the apostrophe appears, followed by a line of minus signs.

Within that text, however, are a few bizarre-looking commands; here's what they mean:

\b\fs24 is a command that says "print this line bold" (that's the b) "and put it in a font size of 24 points" (that's the fs24). It only applies to that line of ASCII text. To make it only apply to just a few characters in a line, then enclose the command and the words in curly braces, as in "this is a {\b\fs24Big Bold Word}." The words "Big Bold Word" would be in 24 point bold.

{\iJurassic Park} says to italicize (that's the \i) the words "Jurassic Park."

[ornithiscian:Ornithiscians] and [sauriscian:Sauriscians] are commands to create jump words. The word "ornithiscian" (say that three times fast) will appear with a solid underline. Clicking on it will cause Help to jump to the topic named *Ornithiscians*. (There must be a topic somewhere named *Ornithiscians*—correct capitalization and all—or this won't work.) The same goes for the word "sauriscian," which will appear with an underline and will cause a jump to a topic names *Sauriscians*.

[[dinosaurs:ddef]] is similar to the jump definition of the words "ornithiscian" and "sauriscian," but the two square brackets say not to create a jump word. Instead, this creates a pop-up reference to a topic named *ddef*.

Next, I'll build each of the other topics in the same way. The entire document then looks like the following listing.

```
\docstart'

\topic About_Dinosaurs'
\keyword introduction'
\keyword contents'
\keyword overview'
\title Null'
\browse General'
========================
\b\fs24 About Dinosaurs'

It's amazing how much the "thunder lizards" (the
Latin meaning of "dinosaur") fascinate us to this
day.
The recent success of {\iJurassic Park} has led
people to think that all of the [[dino-
saurs:ddef]] eventually became birds ... but
that's not completely true. This file explains
the differences between the two different major
families of dinosaurs, the "bird hipped" ([orni-
thiscian:Ornithiscians]) and the "lizard hipped"
([sauriscian:Sauriscians]) dinos.'


------------------------
\topic Sauriscians'
\keyword sauriscian, lizard hipped'
\title Sauriscians (Lizard-Hipped Dinosaurs)'
\browse General'
========================
\b\fs24 Sauriscians (Lizard-Hipped Dinosaurs)'

There were two main kinds (suborders) of lizard-
hipped dinosaurs:'

Therapods, which include the two-legged carnivo-
rous dinosaurs like [[Tyrannosaurus Rex:trex]],
Albertosaurus, and Velociraptor, as well as the
smaller ostrich-like Struthiomimus and Orni-
thomimus herbivores.'
```

Sauropods or sauropodomorphs include Apatosaurus (also known as Brontosaurus), Brachiosaurus, Ultrasaurus, Camarasaurus, and Diplodocus.'

Saurischians lived at the same time as ornithiscians, and probably evolved from a common ancestor in the Triassic period. The early Herrerasaurus and Lesothosaurus are two examples of early dinosaurs that fit into both categories.'

```
------------------------------
\topic Ornithiscians'
\keyword ornithiscian, bird hipped'
\title Ornithiscians (Bird-Hipped Dinosaurs)'
\browse General'
==============================
\b\fs24 Ornithiscians (Bird-Hipped Dinosaurs)'
```

Ornithiscians, or "bird-hipped" dinosaurs, included three suborders:'

Marginocephalia are the horned dinosaurs that number in their ranks Triceratops, Styracosaurus, and Protoceratops.'

Ornithopoda include the duck-billed dinosaurs Trachodon, Maiasaurus, and the crested Parasaurolophus.
Most ornithopods were upright herbivorous animals, and there is evidence that they cared for their young in nests. In the late Cretaceous, these dinosaurs were the most plentiful in North America.'

Thyreophora include the Ankylosaurs and the Stegosaurs, the "plated lizards."'

```
------------------------------
\topic trex'
\keyword Tyrannosaurus Rex'
\title Tyrannosaurus Rex'
```

```
\browse General'
===========================
\b\fs24 Tyrannosaurus Rex'
\bml trex.bmp'
---------------------------
\topic ddef'
\title Dinosaurs Defined'
\browse General'
===========================
The term {\b\fs24Dinosaur} does not, contrary to
popular belief, refer to all prehistoric crea-
tures.
For example the aquatic Plesiosaur and Mosasaur
were not dinosaurs; neither were the flying Ptero-
dactyls. Dinosaur refers only to a particular
group of ancient creature.'
---------------------------

\docend'
```

The topics after the Contents topic are very much like the
Contents topic. The only interesting items are {**\b\fs24Dino-
saurs**} in the *Dinosaurs Defined* topic; that's just a command
to put the word "Dinosaurs" in bold 24-point type. The *Tyrannosaurus Rex* topic has a new command, **\bml;** that displays a bitmap. And, finally, the document ends with a
\docend' command.

Using RTFGEN to Create the Help File

To install RTFGEN, just unzip it and put its files into the
same directory as your copy of the Windows Help Compiler.
(The Windows Help Compiler is available from Microsoft, or
it is also part of the Visual Basic Professional Edition and the
C/C++ Software Development Kit.)

Once you've got your help file written, save it as an ASCII file with the extension TPC. For example, I saved my dinosaurs file as DINOSAUR.TPC. Then start up RTFGEN. You'll see an opening screen like the one shown in Figure 10.8.

FIGURE 10.8

The opening screen of RTFGEN

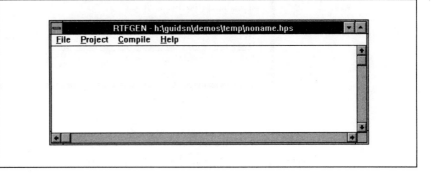

RTFGEN creates "project" files that it uses to keep track of the files associated with a help file. You've got to create one of these project files by clicking File ➤ New. Then click Project ➤ Topic Files. The Topic Source Files dialog box shown in Figure 10.9 appears.

Click Add File and you'll get a dialog box allowing you to choose the DINOSAUR.TPC file. Click OK and you'll be back at the main RTFGEN window. Then click File ➤ Save As, and pick a file name for this project file. You can then click Compile ➤ Full Compile ➤ Display. RTFGEN will check your file to ensure that it follows the RTFGEN language correctly, and then it will invoke the Help Compiler. If all goes well, it will then display your help file.

There's lots more to help files—and lots more that RTFGEN can do—but that's all covered in its documentation. There are a lot of expensive tools for building help, and perhaps they

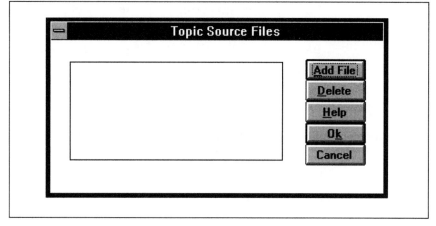

will have some feature that you absolutely must have; when
that happens, then buy them. Until then, get an inexpensive
tool like RTFGEN, and you'll be amazed at what you can do.

Choosing Topics

While this chapter's goal is not to look too deeply into the me-
chanics of building a Windows help file, it is the goal of this
chapter to consider what is important is designing a good, useful help file. With that in mind, consider the tips in the following sections.

Build Two-Way Indexes

Think about the keywords that your user will see in the Search
window that appears in Help, a window like Figure 10.10.

Notice, for example, that both "sauriscian" and "lizard
hipped" are in the Search window. That's because two different people might be looking for the same thing with different
words.

FIGURE **10.10**

The Search window in the Help file

Think of the Search window as your index. Ever been frustrated by an incomplete or inadequate index? Then you'll know how people feel when Search doesn't tell them anything.

Hint: Have someone different from the Help author write the index.

Index Benefits, Not Features

No one cares about features ("supports 16 million-color bitmaps!"); they care about benefits ("you don't have to halftone your bitmaps any more; the software does it automatically!"). Find the benefit keywords ("halftone," "halftone, automatic") and put them in the Search list.

Building Good Help

Make your help really help.

Include Context-Sensitive Help

Take a look at the dialog box shown in Figure 10.11.

FIGURE **10.11**

A dialog box with undefined choices

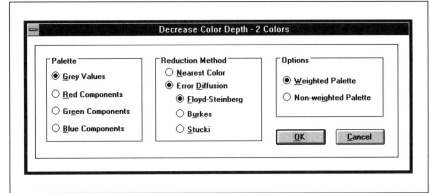

Now, imagine that you're faced with this for the first time. Justwhattheheckisa Stucki Error Diffusion, anyway? I should be able to press F1 and get some advice. Instead, pressing F1 gets me nothing, and canceling and then pressing F1 gets me "Stucki is one of three popular dithering algorithms." Makes you want to run right out and buy this program, doesn't it?

Context-sensitive help requires some extra coding, but it's not too bad. Never offer options like this one unless you're willing to explain them, and explain them correctly. If you don't feel confident about your explanatory powers, hire a technical editor to assist you. Good help is one of those things that separate good programs from programs that look like they were kludged together in someone's basement.

Use Hyperlinks, but Don't Hyper-Do It

The words that show up in green are "hyperlinks." Assuming that "dither" is a word that not all of your users would know, then you should have a "dithering" topic.

But don't just have a "dithering" topic—your audience may not have the patience for that; not everyone's willing to Search for something. Instead, make a hyperlink of the word when it appears in other topics. But only do it once per screen. If it shows up five times in a screen, and every one is green, then there's a bit of sensory overload on your user's part.

Hyperlink to Pop-Ups

If you do hyperlink to terms like "dither," use a pop-up, not a jump.

Use Pictures, Sounds, and Videos

It is now possible to link WAV (sound), BMP (picture), and AVI (moving video/sound) objects into Help files. I didn't have time to do it, but I thought it would be neat to get a clip from *Jurassic Park* and hyperlink it to the *Jurassic Park* reference in my *About Dinosaurs* screen.

Be Lazy and Use a Tool

You've met RTFGEN. There are even easier, if more limited, tools around. I put together a simple help file (25 topics, a few bitmaps) with an inexpensive ($50) authoring tool called

Visual Help. I found it on CompuServe in the WINSHARE forum. There are many things that it cannot do, but you can whip out a help file in a morning...even if you've never done it before.

Don't Mess with "How to Use Help"

Bad though it may be, there is a general Help topic called "How to use Help." Don't improve upon it; it should be uniform across all machines.

Stay with the Basic 16 Colors

Now and then, I see a commercial package that was clearly designed by people with 256-color video boards. They've worked hard to find a very delicate shade of pale yellow background that serves as a perfect counterpoint to the medium blue-gray of the window frame.

Ah, but then I run it in 16-color mode. Little yellow polka-dots against a stark white background, and a muddy blue mess for frames. Not a pretty sight.

Don't stray from the basic 16, and no one will notice. Use special 256-color colors, and people will notice...and decide that they don't like your product.

Be Careful with Graphics

The usual advice about graphics holds: Don't push the envelope, or your fate will be sealed. Keep them simple. Line drawings are good, or simple dithered images. The Help Engine just doesn't handle colors well, even on systems that do have 256 color drivers.

Be Concise

People read more slowly on a screen than they do on paper—30 percent more slowly, according to Microsoft. So they won't read as quickly. Condense your message, so they can get some of that time back.

Keep It Short and Useful

Help topics should never exceed a full VGA screen in size. If it's that complex, break it up. You never want a topic that's anywhere near the size of a screen. Keep the information bite-sized. Again, if you're having trouble organizing the material, hire a freelance technical writer for a few hours. It won't cost much, and it'll greatly improve the product.

Lead Them by the Nose for the First Time

Programs are complex, tempermental beasts that only begin to appear friendly and useful once you've surrendered your preconceived notions and adjusted your thinking to the programmer's mode of thought...or so it seems when you're using someone else's program.

Include a "test flight," or a "sample exercise" in your help files, and people won't call you for tech support. Lead people through a short session where something gets done. Don't just create a document; show people how to save it, retrieve it, print it, and exit the program. Include sample screens in your help files.

Don't Cram: Preserve White Space

I know I said to keep it to a single screen, but white space is important. Be concise, and leave space for a little calming emptiness.

Language Is Important, as Always

All the things we covered in the discussion on using text applies here, and more so: People are often a bit on edge when using Help.

Most People Need Examples

I've got this learning disability—I need examples when things are explained to me. Provide a simple example document, then use it in Help to underscore examples.

I've said it before, but let me close this chapter by reiterating this advice: The help system is one of those things that is by no means necessary, but that you shouldn't skip. CorelDRAW!'s first version lacked help altogether, making it look much more amateurish than its later incarnations. Nowadays, programs with inadequate or nonexistent help look like the program was written by one person, some techno-guru type, with no outside help. If you're a small developer, then it may indeed be the case that you're the only person in your company. But professional software is a joint effort nowadays—if you work alone, you can always temporarily hire staff to fill in your gaps. Intelligent use of freelance graphic designers and technical writers can make a small Visual Basic concoction into a professional-looking application.

CHAPTER 11

LETTING

YOUR

CUSTOMERS

CUSTOMIZE

*T*he reason why you took the time to build a GUI application in the first place was because you felt that it would make your application easy and/or comfortable to use.

The best way to ensure that people are comfortable is to allow them to customize your application, to arrange the furniture and fluff up the pillows in a way that makes them feel like the application was designed for them, and them alone.

There's no deep science to this, just a truly overlooked need. This chapter is mainly, then, a list of suggested locations where virtually every application—probably including *yours*—can be improved by allowing customization.

Directory Customizing

One of the first operations that anyone does with an application, whether using it for the first time or the hundredth time, is to open a file. Make this operation intuitive, and people will get the immediate impression that this is a well thought-out program.

Remember the Last Directory

What directory should the Open operation look to? Well, in order of usefulness:

- Some applications look for files only in the directory that the program itself starts from. This does not allow for data directories to be different from program directories without some extra work. This is the worst arrangement.

- Other applications allow the user to specify a particular file directory. This is better, but it gets annoying if the user wants to retrieve a number of files from a directory that is *not* the default directory; she ends up doing a lot of extra clicking for every file access.

- Even better is to have your File Open dialog remember the last directory that the user read, and to return there with the next File Open command.

Remember the Last File

Along the same lines, imagine that you're examining a series of documents from a very long list. The File Open list box always starts out at the top of a sorted list of files. This can be tremendously tedious when choosing files down toward the bottom of the list. Suggestion: Either implement a telescoping list box, or remember the last access and start from there.

How Long to Remember?

One last thought: Should your application recall the last directory examined from application run to application run? I'd make it an option.

Choosable Colors

Colors, as I've noted earlier, are personal and important. Make it possible to adjust the background and foreground of your application. Use the standard Color dialog box, as your

users already recognize it. It's probably a good idea to use the colors that the user selected from the Control Panel; if we had to separately set colors for each application, that would sort of negate the purpose of the Control Panel's Colors setting.

Options for Application Open Behavior

When an application starts up, it never seems to be exactly ready to get down to work. Either the directory's wrong, or the wrong windows are open, or....

The perfect application sets things up the way your user left them when he closed the application down; but, recognizing that sometimes the reason why the application was closed down in the first place was because it wasn't working, the perfect application *also* has an escape hatch that will restore things to a "vanilla" setting or, even better, roll back the previous actions one at a time.

Include options that allow an application to start up in any one of these modes:

- With an empty screen. Excel is annoying in that getting it to start up with no "SHEET1" in its window is not easy.

- With a particular document, perhaps the last one that your user worked on.

- Running some kind of "autostart" macro, assuming that your application supports a macro language.

- Minimized, maximized, or windowed. If windowed, where the window should go. Additionally, the window should be smart enough to know if the screen resolution has changed and the window is no longer visible—in which case it should move itself somewhere where it *is* visible.

Data Display Options

As text and graphics require some time to display, you should offer the option to show the data as "greeked" text, the graphics as boxes, and the sounds as speaker icons.

For anything involving more than one page of data, a zoom feature is wonderful.

Modularize for Size

Not everyone's got dozens of megabytes of memory. Build the program to be modular and give the user the option to discard modules so as to be able to get down to a configuration of minimum RAM impact.

Similarly, allow your users to know how much memory your program—and the options that they've enabled—require. Knowing that keeping the spell checker active is costing 1.5 MB might help them figure out how to get more memory when things are tight.

Exploit the Right Mouse Button

Give people some way to use the right mouse button. Why not show your user the entire menu, and allow her to assign one menu item to the right mouse button?

Control Confirmations

All those "are you sure?" dialog boxes are a great idea when you're just getting started, but after a while they get pretty annoying. Offer the ability to disable the "are you sure?" boxes for:

- exiting the application
- exiting a document that hasn't been saved
- overwriting a file.

Toolbars

If your application uses toolbars or multiple windows, make it possible to specify whether or not these objects appear on the screen at startup, and make it possible for them to be added or subtracted from the screen at any moment.

If using toolbars, make them customizable. They are supposed to be convenient, and simply saying, "Here's my programmer's idea of convenience—take it or leave it" makes no sense. Toolbars are quite expensive in terms of screen real estate and in Windows resources; make them worthwhile, or get rid of them.

Fonts

For this last item, I'm going to run counter to my own advice and suggest that you *not* make fonts customizable. Dialog boxes, menus, and other objects that contain text should retain their default fonts.

If you *do* make fonts customizable, then be sure to add some logic to your program that checks screen resolution at runtime to make sure that text isn't clipped.

The difference between programs from the "old days" and modern programs is that we developers are devoting more CPU cycles to making programs more comfortable to work with. But there's not a real consensus on exactly *how* far to customize an application. As a result, you're in partially uncharted territory when designing options into your program. My final piece of advice here is to simply provide customization features that stay out of the way until you need them.

WRAPPING

IT

UP:

LAYING

OUT

YOUR

GUI

APPLICATION

*B*efore we part, this brief chapter discusses some suggested steps to designing a GUI application. If you've never built a GUI application before, I believe that you'll find these tips useful.

Prototyping

It is still possible to build a program from scratch using just a C or C++ compiler, a Software Development Kit (SDK) and lots of blood, toil, tears, and sweat. In fact, I'm sure that it's being done in hundreds of programming shops at this very moment.

Two programmers named David E.Y. Sarna and George J. Febish have written a book called *Windows Rapid Application Development*, published by Ziff-Davis Press. It discusses a technique for GUI development that they call MARVEL. The letters in the name stand for:

- **M**odular programming, which exhorts you to build reusable tools and *shareable* tools like Dynamic Link Libraries (DLLs).

- **A**utomatic interfaces: make it possible for your program to be invoked by another program via something like Dynamic Data Exchange (DDE) or Object Linking and Embedding (OLE). In the OS/2 world, that would mean building objects that fit into the System Object Model (SOM). "Automatic" interfaces here should be compared to "human" interfaces—that is, the programmer.

- Rethinking programming, which just means "refer to the other things in this list."

- Visual development environments make programming faster.

- Extensible languages refers to those that can grow through object orientation and extended controls like the ones that you see in Visual Basic.

- Linking refers to DLLs and OLE again; I guess they wanted to make sure that the acronym spelled something.

Sarna and Febish's basic idea has a lot of merit: Use the power of the GUI interface and the underlying operating system. Our users don't look at programs with clunky character-based interfaces like they did in 1975, so stop writing code the way people did in 1975— use visual development tools.

Prototyping Tools

I'm about to get laughed at, but I'll say this anyway.

Think seriously about using a visual tool like Visual Basic to develop your application.

The great thing about Visual Basic is that you can prototype a system using it, show it to the user, and change the user interface right on the fly to accommodate the user! You can't believe how happy customers are to see you making their requested changes right in front of their face.

Why doesn't everybody use VB? Three reasons:

- It's perceived as being Basic, which is bad;

- It's perceived as being slow;
- People attack projects the wrong way using it.

There's a long-standing prejudice against Basic; Visual Basic has inherited that prejudice. I wish that Microsoft had named it something different. The original Basics were all interpreted and slow, so that reputation has carried down through the years.

It's a partially valid argument: VB *is* interpreted. Doing computations in it is a very bad idea. But that's not what VB is all about. VB is all about building front-ends.

That brings me to the third mistake that people make about VB: They use it wrong, if they use it at all. As I just said, it's interpreted. Computing Mandelbrot sets isn't a very good idea with VB (although my technical editor comments that *he* wrote a fractal generator in VB that ran about as fast as one he wrote in C++). What *is* a good idea is to write the data-grinding part of your application in whatever language you like, whether it's C, FORTRAN, COBOL, or whatever, and then make that code into a DLL. *Then* call those compiled, fast routines from your VB-designed front end.

What I've just described sounds hard, but it isn't. We've been isolating program sections for decades now; keeping them in different languages is really not difficult. And many compilers nowadays support the DLL format.

If worse comes to worst, you can always use VB as a prototyping tool, then rewrite the GUI part in a more difficult, traditional tool.

Visual Basic

VB's my first choice for quick prototyping tools, as I've said. Microsoft keeps improving it, and intends eventually to wrap it into Windows somehow as a kind of "super macro language." When I've needed a sample dialog box or window as an illustration for writing this book, I've relied exclusively upon Visual Basic.

VB can't do everything. For example, it's difficult to synchronize external events with VB. By that, I mean that it's hard in VB to say, "Wait until Paintbrush is finished printing before doing this," because of the nature of Windows.

Perhaps VB's greatest strength is its extensibility. Dozens of companies have created new tools for VB, tools that fit seamlessly into its visual development environment.

PubTech WinBatch/Norton Batch Builder

For even simpler uses, you might look at PubTech's product, which is incorporated into the Norton Desktop for Windows. It's a batch language for controlling Windows.

It even includes a dialog-box editor, and will produce EXE files with a $100 add-on piece of software available from Pub-Tech. A word of warning, however: Its default look and feel is pretty ugly. You'll have to smack it around a bit to get your PubTech creations to look like standard Windows applications. The main use I'd get out of this would be simple creation of installation programs.

Asymmetrix Toolbook

Toolbook is a very nifty GUI-prototyping tool. It's somewhat like Visual Basic, but does not produce code that is as fast. Toolbook is, however, a more flexible language, and its similarities to VB make it easy to move between languages. It will not create a stand-alone EXE file, which is a disadvantage.

Toolbook also will not create DLLs or Windows objects. The tools that you build with Toolbook cannot be accessed outside of Toolbook, crippling it considerably.

That about wraps this little guide up. I hope I've given you a few things to think about, spared you a few egregious goofs, and maybe "charged you up" for some new GUI programming. We *need* good GUI programs, so fire up that development tool, measure those dialog box units, and—as I said in the beginning—go out and make something beautiful!

Boldface page numbers indicate definitions and principal discussions of topics. *Italic* page numbers indicate illustrations.

A CLEVER GUIDE TO FOXPRO PROGRAMMING.

700 pp. ISBN: 1217-1.

*P*rogrammer's Guide to FoxPro 2.5 is a straightforward, highly focused tutorial guide to using Fox-Pro 2.5 to develop business systems. As you follow step-by-step instructions in the book, you'll learn the essentials of FoxPro programming.

Learn how to design data tables and data entry screens for Customer, Sales and Payment data. Create a Windows-style interface to help you make FoxPro more productive. You'll even find tips for using the FoxPro Report Writer and Label Writer to create forms.

All of this and more is included on a FREE disk that walks you through the development of a full-featured, sample accounts-receivable system. This book is perfect for Xbase developers making their move to Windows.

SYBEX. Help Yourself.

2021 Challenger Drive
Alameda, CA 94501
1-510-523-8233
1-800-227-2346

SYBEX

SMOOTH SAILING FOR CLIPPER PROGRAMMERS.

1,200pp. ISBN: 1097-5.

SYBEX

YES, YOU *CAN* DO WINDOWS.

A NEW VIEW THROUGH YOUR WINDOWS.

150pp. ISBN: 1119-X.

YOUR GUIDE TO DOS DOMINANCE.

GET A FREE CATALOG JUST FOR EXPRESSING YOUR OPINION.

Help us improve our books and get a *FREE* full-color catalog in the bargain. Please complete this form, pull out this page and send it in today. The address is on the reverse side.

Name _____   **Company** _____

Address _____   **City** _____ **State** ____ **Zip** _____

Phone (___) _____

1. How would you rate the overall quality of this book?

❑ Excellent
❑ Very Good
❑ Good
❑ Fair
❑ Below Average
❑ Poor

2. What were the things you liked most about the book? (Check all that apply)

❑ Pace
❑ Format
❑ Writing Style
❑ Examples
❑ Table of Contents
❑ Index
❑ Price
❑ Illustrations
❑ Type Style
❑ Cover
❑ Depth of Coverage
❑ Fast Track Notes

3. What were the things you liked *least* about the book? (Check all that apply)

❑ Pace
❑ Format
❑ Writing Style
❑ Examples
❑ Table of Contents
❑ Index
❑ Price
❑ Illustrations
❑ Type Style
❑ Cover
❑ Depth of Coverage
❑ Fast Track Notes

4. Where did you buy this book?

❑ Bookstore chain
❑ Small independent bookstore
❑ Computer store
❑ Wholesale club
❑ College bookstore
❑ Technical bookstore
❑ Other _____

5. How did you decide to buy this particular book?

❑ Recommended by friend
❑ Recommended by store personnel
❑ Author's reputation
❑ Sybex's reputation
❑ Read book review in _____
❑ Other _____

6. How did you pay for this book?

❑ Used own funds
❑ Reimbursed by company
❑ Received book as a gift

7. What is your level of experience with the subject covered in this book?

❑ Beginner
❑ Intermediate
❑ Advanced

8. How long have you been using a computer?

years _____
months _____

9. Where do you most often use your computer?

❑ Home
❑ Work

❑ Both
❑ Other _____

10. What kind of computer equipment do you have? (Check all that apply)

❑ PC Compatible Desktop Computer
❑ PC Compatible Laptop Computer
❑ Apple/Mac Computer
❑ Apple/Mac Laptop Computer
❑ CD ROM
❑ Fax Modem
❑ Data Modem
❑ Scanner
❑ Sound Card
❑ Other _____

11. What other kinds of software packages do you ordinarily use?

❑ Accounting
❑ Databases
❑ Networks
❑ Apple/Mac
❑ Desktop Publishing
❑ Spreadsheets
❑ CAD
❑ Games
❑ Word Processing
❑ Communications
❑ Money Management
❑ Other _____

12. What operating systems do you ordinarily use?

❑ DOS
❑ OS/2
❑ Windows
❑ Apple/Mac
❑ Windows NT
❑ Other _____

13. On what computer-related subject(s) would you like to see more books?

_____

_____

_____

_____

14. Do you have any other comments about this book? (Please feel free to use a separate piece of paper if you need more room)

_____

_____

_____

_____

- - - - - - - - - - - - - - PLEASE FOLD, SEAL, AND MAIL TO SYBEX - - - - - - - - - - - - -

SYBEX INC.
Department M
2021 Challenger Drive
Alameda, CA
94501